CW00727477

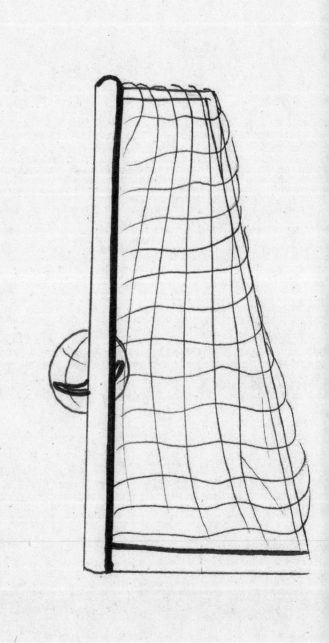

100 FACTS

Man City

First published in Great Britain in 2015
by Wymer Publishing
www.wymerpublishing.co.uk
Wymer Publishing is a trading name of Wymer (UK) Ltd

First edition. Copyright © 2013 Steve Horton / Wymer Publishing.

ISBN 978-1-908724-14-4

Edited by John Kemp.

Typeset by Wymer.
Printed and bound by Clays, Bungay, Suffolk.

A catalogue record for this book is available from the British Library.

Cover design by Wymer.
Sketches by Becky Welton. © 2014.

100
FACTS

Man City

Steve Horton

WYMER
WP
PUBLISHING

Bedford, England

1880
ST MARK'S
FORMED

The football club that would eventually become Manchester City was formed in 1880 and stemmed from a church cricket club.

In 1875 William Beastow, a Churchwarden at St Mark's Church in Clowes Street (now occupied by a row of shops), formed the cricket club to give local unemployed men something to do and stop them getting involved in criminality. Although St Mark's was a Protestant church the club was open to men of all faiths.

In 1880 Beastow and another Churchwarden, Thomas Goodbehere decided to start a football club to give the members a sport to play in winter. The first game was at home against a Baptist Church side from Macclesfield on 13 November 1880, with St Mark's losing 2-1. The exact site of the pitch is not certain, although the game is commonly believed to have been played on wasteland off Thomas Street, with the players changing in the church hall beforehand.

It is not known exactly how many friendlies were played in that first season, although the first victory came against Stalybridge Clarence in March. St Mark's then moved to Kirkmanshulme Cricket Club in Redgate Lane for 1881-82, before moving to land off Queen's Road that is now the site of Gorton Park.

1882
FIRST VICTORY VERSUS MANCHESTER UNITED

The origins of the Manchester derby go back to the 1881-82 season when the two clubs that eventually became Manchester City and Manchester United played each other twice.

The first match between St Mark's and Newton Heath (United's name until 1902) took place on 12 November 1881 at the 'Heathens' North Road ground, with the home side winning 3-0.

On 4 March 1882 a return fixture took place at Kirkmanshulme and attracted a healthy crowd of 5,000, even though there was no special significance in the fixture as there were many other clubs in Manchester at the time.

St Mark's took an eighth minute lead and were 2-0 up by half time, the second goal being a fine solo effort by Collinge, who had ran the length of the pitch after collecting the ball just outside his own penalty area.

Newton Heath managed a late consolation goal in what turned out to be the last game St Mark's played at Kirkmanshulme. At the end of the season they moved out as the cricket club were unhappy at the damage that football was causing to their pitch.

1884
ST MARK'S
BECOME GORTON

In 1884 a split occurred in St Mark's with two different clubs being formed. The club had continued to play friendlies at Queen's Road for the previous two seasons but in 1884 a divide occurred between players still connected to St Mark's and those that had joined since its formation.

Newer players formed West Gorton Athletic and continued to play at Queen's Road, leaving the old St Mark's members to find a new ground. Under the new name of Gorton AFC, they agreed a rent of £6 per year on some land off Pink Bank Lane.

This move proved to be a temporary measure and had probably come out of desperation to have anywhere that would do as a home ground due to the split. The move didn't do their form any harm though, as in sixteen games in 1884-85 Gorton won seven, drew seven and lost two.

For 1885-86 Gorton moved to land next to the Bull's Head Hotel on Reddish Lane. Their first game there was a 1-1 draw with Earlstown on 3 October 1885. A pub of this name exists today on the site, although it is not the original one from the 1880s.

1887
ON THE MOVE AGAIN
AS GORTON BECOME ARDWICK

After just two years at the Bull's Head, Gorton AFC were on the move and changing their name again.

At the end of 1886-87 the landlord of the Bull's Head asked for more rent which the Committee were reluctant to pay. Club captain Kenneth McKenzie found some waste land close to his workplace that was owned by the Manchester, Sheffield and Lincolnshire Railway Company.

The Committee members took some convincing as to the land's potential as a football ground due to its polluted state. However they also knew that in moving to the new ground Gorton would be closer to St Mark's Church than any of the other places they had played at, except for the very first one.

The ground was levelled off by August and with it being located in Ardwick, the committee decided to change the name of the club to reflect this. For the first few seasons the facilities were very basic, with the first seats only being installed in 1888 and players changing at the Hyde Road Hotel until 1896.

What Hyde Road did provide though was potential to allow the club to grow, something that would become very important with the onset of professionalism at the time and the formation of the Football League being imminent.

1889
THE FIRST FLOODLIT
MANCHESTER DERBY

The first floodlit match to take place in Manchester was on 26 February 1889 when Ardwick took on Newton Heath to raise funds following a mining disaster.

The match was arranged after 23 miners were killed in an explosion at the Hyde Road colliery on 18th January. It was played at the Belle Vue athletic ground and the pitch was lit using a number of Wells electric lamps, which were powered by paraffin and usually used in the construction industry. Newton Heath won 3-2 in front of a crowd of 10,000.

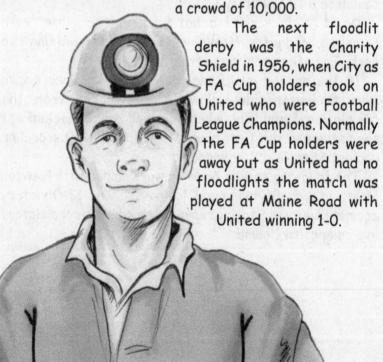

The next floodlit derby was the Charity Shield in 1956, when City as FA Cup holders took on United who were Football League Champions. Normally the FA Cup holders were away but as United had no floodlights the match was played at Maine Road with United winning 1-0.

1890
ARDWICK'S FIRST FA CUP SCORE REMAINS A RECORD

Ardwick's first venture into the FA Cup saw them win their opening game 12-0, a result that remains Manchester City's record victory.

Ardwick entered in the competition at the first qualifying round stage and were drawn against little known Liverpool Stanley, with the game being played on 4th October.

4,000 turned up at Hyde Road and Ardwick attacked from the start, building up a 5-0 half time lead. After the break there was no let up and they added seven more to complete a 12-0 victory.

David Weir scored a hat-trick in the game, with Campbell, Hodgetts, McWhinnie and Rushton getting two each. The other goal came from Whittle.

In the second qualifying round Ardwick were drawn away to Bolton side Halliwell but withdrew from the completion. Ironically, when Halliwell were knocked out themselves in the first round, it was by a 12-0 scoreline against Sheffield Wednesday.

The following season Ardwick were paired with Newton Heath in a qualifying round, losing 5-1. The 12-0 victory against Liverpool Stanley remains the club's record victory in a competitive game.

1892
ELECTION TO THE
FOOTBALL LEAGUE

Ardwick were elected to the Football League in 1892 when it was extended and a Second Division formed.

The Football League had been formed in 1888 and initially consisted of twelve clubs, which was expanded to fourteen in 1891. That same year Ardwick had joined the Football Alliance, founded in 1889 as a rival to the Football League but realistically consisting of clubs who weren't as strong.

With Laurence Furniss as manager, Ardwick finished eighth in 1891-92 and at the end of that season it was agreed that the two leagues would merge, although it was effectively a takeover with a Second Division of the Football League being formed to which Alliance clubs needed to be elected.

Three of the strongest clubs from the Football Alliance – Newton Heath, Nottingham Forest and The Wednesday were elected to the First Division which was expanded to sixteen teams. Darwen, who had finished bottom of the Football League in 1890-91, were elected into the Second Division.

All of the remaining Football Alliance clubs were elected to the Second Division along with newcomers Burslem Port Vale, Northwich Victoria and Sheffield United.

Ardwick made an excellent start to the 1892-93 season, beating Bootle 7-0 at home on 3rd September and winning five of their first six games. However despite being top at the end of October they struggled afterwards and lost eight out of ten games played after New Year to eventually finish fifth.

1894
ARDWICK BECOMES MANCHESTER CITY

At the end of the 1893-94 season, Ardwick FC was no more as the name was changed to Manchester City.

The club finished second to bottom of the Second Division that season and was in serious financial trouble. For one game, away to Crewe in February they were unable to raise a full team and played with ten players.

The club effectively wound itself up and reformed as a public limited company with a new name, Manchester City, on the last day of the season. It was hoped that by changing the name the club could attract support from the city as a whole not just the Ardwick and east Manchester area.

The name change soon paid off as City finished ninth in 1894-95. Crowds were also much higher than the season before, with the 1893-94 best of 6,000 being bettered on four occasions.

1894
WELSH CUP WINNING
MINER JOINS

One of the newly re-branded Manchester City's first signings was Northwich Victoria's Billy Meredith, although he refused to give up his day job.

Meredith hailed from the North Wales town of Chirk and had first gone down the pit at the age of twelve in 1884. Between 1892 and 1894 he turned out occasionally for Northwich, who paid his expenses, as well as winning the Welsh Cup with his local side Chirk AAA.

When Northwich withdrew from the Football League at the end of 1893-94 City officials travelled to Chirk but were met with opposition from his mother who believed he should have a steady job and play football for his amusement.

Meredith initially played for City as an amateur, making his debut against Newcastle on 27 October 1894, a game City lost 5-4. The following week he made his home debut against Newton Heath in the first match between the two sides in the Football League. City lost 5-2, but Meredith scored both goals and before the end of the season he had given up his mining job and turned professional.

Meredith was City's top scorer in both 1894-95 and 1895-96, despite playing on the wing. He captained City to their first FA Cup win in 1904 and in eleven years scored 129 goals in 339 league appearances. He joined Manchester United in 1906 after he was suspended by City following a bribery scandal, but would later be back at Hyde Road.

FACT 10
BEST GOALS TALLY
IN A LEAGUE GAME

The most number of goals Manchester City have scored in a league game was on 23 March 1895 when they hammered Lincoln City 11-3 at Hyde Road.

City were tenth in the league going into the game with thirteenth-placed Lincoln. But form meant City were clear favourites. They had won their last four games at Hyde Road, while Lincoln had lost their last eight away, including a 7-1 mauling at Port Vale a week earlier.

City were superior in every department and led 5-1 at half time, scoring six more in the second half to win 11-3. Wally McReddie scored four of City's goals and Pat Finnerhan, Billy Meredith and Sandy Rowan got two each, with Bob Milarvie getting the other.

Although City have enjoyed greater margins of victory, this remains the only time they have scored eleven goals in a league game. It is also the only time that fourteen goals have been scored in a match in English football's second tier.

1896
CITY LOSE OUT
IN TEST MATCHES

In 1895-96 Manchester City came close to promotion when they finished second in the Second Division but lost out in the test matches that were played to determine promotion and relegation.

Managed by Sam Ormerord, City were consistent all season, winning nine of their first eleven games and never being out of the top three. At Hyde Road they were unbeaten, winning twelve and drawing three of their fifteen games, with local rivals Newton Heath being beaten 2-1.

Despite their excellent form City were pushed all the way by Burton Wanderers and they only secured a place in the test matches on the last day of the season with a 2-0 win at home to Notts County.

The test matches consisted of a series of games involving City and Second Division Champions Liverpool against Small Heath (now Birmingham City) and West Bromwich Albion, who had finished in the bottom two places of the First Division. City needed to finish in the top two of the group but even that wouldn't secure promotion, as they would then need to be elected to the First Division by the other members.

Although City's excellent home form continued as they drew 1-1 with West Brom and beat Small Heath 3-0, away from home they were well beaten. They lost 6-1 at Small Heath and 8-0 against West Brom, meaning they finished third in the table and had to be content with Second Division football again the following season.

1899
BIGGEST
LEAGUE VICTORY

Manchester City's biggest ever league victory came on 18 February 1899 when Darwen were beaten 10-0 at Hyde Road.

Going into the game City were top of the league and Darwen bottom, having lost nine of their ten away games to date, conceding 56 goals.

On a fine day Darwen offered little resistance, but at half time City were only 3-0 up thanks to goals from Billy Meredith, George Dougal and Fred Williams. In the second half Darwen played even worse and Williams got four more, while Meredith also weighed in with three more to make it 10-0, maintaining City's one point lead at the top.

Things got no better for Darwen as they also lost 10-0 in their next away game, at Walsall. The City defeat was one of eighteen in succession, a record that remains today and at the end of the season they left the Football League.

Since then City have managed to score ten goals in league games, most famously in a 10-1 win against Huddersfield in 1987-88, but they haven't been able to secure a ten goal winning margin.

1899
FIRST TEAM TO BE
PROMOTED AUTOMATICALLY

Three years after missing out in the test matches, Manchester City won promotion to the First Division in 1898-99 becoming the first team to go up by this route.

The previous season the test matches had descended into a farce when Stoke and Burnley, knowing that a draw would be enough to secure top flight status for both of them, drew 0-0 with neither side having a shot at goal. Although there was no direct evidence of collusion the Football League decided to scrap this system in favour of automatic promotion and relegation on a two up two down basis.

Although City began the season with a 7-2 thrashing of Grimsby at Hyde Road they didn't win any of their next three games, which included a 3-0 defeat at Newton Heath. On 1st October they beat Woolwich Arsenal (now Arsenal) 3-1 at home, the first of a thirteen game unbeaten sequence that stretched to Boxing Day.

On 2nd January, City had a disappointing 2-0 home defeat against Glossop which left it very tight at the top, with just three points separating first placed City with Leicester, who were fifth. The following week though City won 1-0 at second placed New Brighton Tower, starting a sequence of four wins and a draw from five games that saw them open up a four point gap over third placed Port Vale.

City's last defeat of the season was at Gainsborough Trinity on 25th February. They then won eight and drew two of the last ten games, scoring 26 goals and conceding just four. Promotion was secured on 8 April 1899 when they beat Small Heath 2-0 at home in the third from last game. This made City the first club to secure automatic promotion with six teams still harbouring hope of the second spot, which was eventually secured by Glossop.

1903
PROMOTED BACK
AT THE FIRST ATTEMPT

After suffering relegation in 1902 Manchester City were promoted back to the top flight after just one season in the Second Division.

City lost just one of their first eight games to go top of the table at the end of October. However, the disappointment of having a game against Barnsley abandoned while they were 5-0 up saw a slight wobble in which two of the next three games were lost and they slipped to fourth.

City then won eight out of nine games up until New Year, including a 3-2 win in the re-arranged game against Barnsley. They returned to the top in the middle of December and were never off it, with a draw and defeat in successive away games in January still leaving them four points clear of third place Arsenal.

Between 24th January and 17th March, City won six games in succession scoring 35 goals, a run that included a 7-1 victory against Port Vale and 9-0 win over Gainsborough Trinity. City's home form was devastating that season, with fifteen out of the seventeen games at Hyde Road being won and 64 goals scored.

Promotion was sealed in the fourth from last game, a 2-0 win over Stockport at Edgeley Park, with leading scorer Billie Gillespie getting the opening goal. The following week the unbeaten home record was spoilt when Manchester United won 2-0 at Hyde Road, but City won their last two games to finish the season as Second Division Champions, three points ahead of second placed Small Heath.

1904
THE GREATEST NORTH TO SOUTH EXODUS FOR CUP FINAL

In 1904 Manchester City won the FA Cup for the first time, beating Bolton 1-0 in the first final contested between two Lancashire clubs.

After winning promotion City had a fantastic 1903-04 season and were always challenging for the title. Going into the final, a Double was a possibility as City topped the table although they had played one game more than second placed Sheffield Wednesday, who were a point behind.

City had a difficult route to the final, playing a First Division side in every round bar one. In the quarter final Hyde Road's biggest crowd to date of 35,000 saw them draw 0-0 with Middlesbrough, before they won the replay 3-1.

City were widely tipped to beat Second Division Bolton in the final, for which 30,000 travelled from Lancashire to London. The *Manchester Evening News* said it was the largest number of people ever to travel by rail from the north to south of England and many fans slept on the platforms at Euston and St Pancras stations due to lack of accommodation.

City won the game 1-0 thanks to a 23rd minute goal from Billy Meredith and apart from a brief spell in the second half they were in control for most of the game.

The FA Cup victory was City's first major honour but they couldn't make it a double as two days later they lost 1-0 at Everton, which confirmed Sheffield Wednesday as Football League Champions.

1906
NEW LOOK TEAM FINISHED
FIRST GAME WITH SIX MEN

On the first day of the 1906-07 season a depleted Manchester City were beaten 4-1 by Woolwich Arsenal on what is believed to be the hottest day that football has been played in England.

City had been forced to sell off most of their best players during the summer to pay fines that had been imposed after the club were found guilty of paying illegal bonuses to players. The FA investigation came about after Billy Meredith, found guilty of offering an opponent a bribe to lose a game, went public with what was happening after City refused to help him financially during his own period of suspension.

City were very much scapegoats for what was going on in the game as a whole, with manager Tom Maley stating that if every club was investigated in the same way "not four would come out scatheless." Maley himself was suspended from football for life and Harry Newbould appointed manager.

It meant that against Woolwich Arsenal five players made their debuts, including the goalkeeper and three of the five forwards. In temperatures of 32.2 degrees Celsius, the highest known for a football match in England, City found themselves 2-0 down at half time. To make matters worse, Jimmy Conlin, Bob Grieve and Irvine Thornley were unable to continue and City began the second half playing a 1-3-3 formation.

Five minutes after the restart Conlin came back onto the pitch and set up a goal for George Dorsett, who collapsed soon afterwards and had to be taken off. He was soon joined by James Buchan and Thomas Kelso, leaving City with just five fit men and the struggling Conlin. The referee saw no reason to abandon the game but Arsenal didn't take too much advantage, scoring just twice more.

RELEGATED AFTER BEING OUT OF BOTTOM TWO ALL SEASON

FACT 17

In 1909 Manchester City suffered a surprising relegation from the First Division, not entering the drop zone until after the very last match of the season.

City had finished third in 1907-08 and although they made an inconsistent start to the next season, winning four and losing four of the first ten games, there was still no sign of what was to come. In November and December they improved with five wins out of seven, the highlight being a 6-1 home win over Bury and going into the New Year they were seventh. This form continued into January and although there was disappointment when City lost away to Manchester United, the following week they beat Everton, who would eventually finish second, 4-0 at home.

The slump that would lead to relegation started on 20th February with a 5-1 defeat at Notts County. This was followed by defeats to Newcastle and Leicester that saw City drop to fourteenth after they had lost three games running for the first time that season. They picked themselves up again though and won successive home games 4-0 against Sheffield Wednesday and Liverpool to move up to tenth with five matches left.

When City beat Nottingham Forest 2-1 at Hyde Road on 13th April they looked to be out of danger, five points clear of nineteenth placed Bradford. They then lost their last three games, the last of which was on 28th April and agonisingly this meant that they were seventeenth but knew two other teams who hadn't yet completed their fixtures could over haul them. The following day Bradford City beat Manchester united and then on 30th April Liverpool won 1-0 at Champions Newcastle to condemn City to the drop on goal average.

1910
PROMOTED BACK
AT FIRST ATTEMPT

Just like 1902 City were promoted straight back to the top flight at the first attempt. Beaten 2-1 at home to Blackpool in their first game they lost only one of the next eleven matches and they were second at the end of October. However a 1-0 defeat at Oldham on 13th November followed by a 1-1 at Fulham saw them drop to fifth.

A 4-0 win over Burnley on 4th December was the start of a run of ten wins in eleven games over the next three months that took City to the top of the table. However they couldn't open any gap as the form of their rivals was so good, with just two points separating the top four teams. A 0-0 draw with Barnsley on 9th March saw City drop to second and the following week they were beaten 3-1 at leaders Derby, but still had a three point gap on third placed Leicester.

Over the Easter weekend City missed a great chance to open up a big gap on new challengers Oldham, who came to Hyde Road and won 2-0. A slump by Derby meant City went top of the table with a 3-0 win at Glossop on 6th April and their good form continued as they won five and drew two out of their next seven games.

In the penultimate game Leeds City were beaten 3-0 at Hyde Road, leaving City top of the table but knowing Hull and Derby could both still overhaul them. However City were able to begin their celebrations early when on 28th April Derby could only draw at Glossop. This meant that the only way City could fail to be promoted was if they lost their last game at Wolves, and Derby won by more than fifteen goals at West Bromwich Albion! City lost 3-2 at Wolves but Derby drew 0-0 at West Brom, meaning City were promoted as Champions, with Oldham sneaking into second spot.

UNITED MANAGER
CELEBRATES CITY DERBY WIN

FACT 19

When Manchester City beat Manchester United 1-0 early in the 1912-13 season, United's manager was pleased with the victory as he had agreed to take over at City.

Ernest Mangnall had been at United since 1903, winning two league titles and an FA Cup, as well as instigating their move to Old Trafford. Despite his success there, City persuaded him to take over at Hyde Road but when the two clubs met at Old Trafford on 7th September, he still hadn't taken up his position even though it was known he had agreed to join.

City won 1-0 despite playing most of the game with ten men and some press reports stated that Mangnall was rejoicing even though he was still technically United's manager.

Mangnall moved into his office at Hyde Road the following Monday and continued City's good start to the season, winning the next three games to make it five in succession overall. However, after being top at Christmas, City suffered a loss of form and they eventually finished sixth.

The First World War interrupted Mangnall's City managerial career but when league football resumed they continued to play attractive football, often leading to lock outs at Hyde Road but he was unable to bring any trophy success.

Mangnall didn't have his contract renewed at the end of 1923-24 and he went on to have a role in the Professional Footballers Association.

1920
THE KING ATTENDS
HOME GAME

In 1920 history was created when a reigning monarch visited a match outside of London for the first time as King George V watched Manchester City's game against Liverpool at Hyde Road.

The match was played on 27th March and the day before, the King was in Liverpool attending the Grand National horse race. On the morning of the game he attended various institutions in Manchester before arriving at Hyde Road ten minutes before the 3.15pm kick off.

The 'club gossip' notes in the programme for the match commented on how great an honour it was to have the King at the match, stating: *Today will for ever be memorable in the annals of our club, and will long be cherished by our supporters by reason of the presence of His Majesty THE KING. It is a historic*

occasion and we have a deep sense of great honour which has been conferred upon our club.

The King was escorted onto the pitch by the City Chairman Mr J.E. Chapman whilst the National Anthem was played. He was then introduced to the players of both sides in the centre circle before watching the match from the Directors' Box alongside the Lord Mayor.

City won the game 2-1 thanks to two goals from Horace Barnes. Immediately afterwards, the King was taken to London Road station from where he returned to London by special train.

1921
TWO YEAR UNBEATEN
HOME RUN COMES TO END

When league football resumed after the end of the First World War Manchester City went on a 42 game run that saw them unbeaten at Hyde Road for two years.

On 6 December 1919 City lost 3-2 at home to eventual Champions West Bromwich Albion, then in their next home game on Christmas Day drew 1-1 with Everton. They then won nine successive home games, before drawing the last two. Unfortunately City's away form was dire and they lost five in succession during March and April, and finished seventh in the league.

The following season City were almost invincible at home, winning nineteen and drawing two of their 21 home league games as they finished second. The sequence included a 3-0 home win over Manchester United and also a 3-0 victory over Burnley that ended their sequence of thirty games unbeaten from the start of the season, which was then a record. Burnley finished that season as Champions, five points ahead of City whose away form again let them down as twelve games on the road were lost.

In 1921-22 City avoided defeat in their first eight home games, which included a 4-1 win over Manchester United. On 3 December 1921, Bolton won 3-1 at Hyde Road bringing an end to the sequence. In addition to 41 league games without defeat, City also played one FA Cup tie during this period, beating Leyton Orient on 10 January 1920 making the sequence 42 in total.

In 1923 Manchester City left Hyde Road after 36 years to move to a new ground at Maine Road.

Ernest Mangnall's side were attracting large crowds and Hyde Road's 40,000 capacity was often stretched to the limit, with a fire in the main stand in 1920 leaving City with some big decisions to make about the future.

City initially approached United about sharing Old Trafford but were quoted excessive terms, while nearby Belle Vue offered the same capacity restrictions as Hyde Road did. In 1922 City announced that they would be moving away from East Manchester to Moss Side, where they could build a much larger stadium, which Mangnall termed an 'English Hampden.'

City moved into what was the largest club ground in England in September 1923, with the capacity set at 80,000 but with the potential to be increased to 120,000. The stadium had one 10,000 seat grandstand and terracing on the other three sides. Initially it had been suggested that it be named after Chairman Lawrence Furniss, but he felt it inappropriate that a living person have the ground named after them so Maine Road was settled on.

In 1923-24 76,166 attended an FA Cup tie with Cardiff which was the largest football crowd seen in Manchester at the time and fully justified Mangnall's calls to move away form Hyde Road.

1924
CITY'S
OLDEST PLAYER

Billy Meredith became Manchester City's oldest player in 1924, making his last appearance for the club thirty years after his first one.

After spending fifteen years at Manchester United, Meredith re-joined City at the age of 47 in 1921, re-uniting with his old manager Ernest Mangall. He made 25 appearances in 1921-22 but failed to score as City finished tenth in the table.

Over the next two seasons he played only seven more times, but four of these came in the FA Cup in 1923-24. Coincidentally his last game for City came against Newcastle, the same team he had made his debut against way back in 1894.

Meredith was 49 years 245 days old when he played in that game, which was an FA Cup semi-final that took place at Birmingham City's St Andrew's ground. Meredith was unable to inspire City to victory as Newcastle won 2-0, with the *Daily Express* reporting that, *he did some things to draw applause from the crowd, but it was apparent that the 'hurly burly of cup tie warfare' was not for someone his age.*

At the end of 1923-24 Meredith retired and he briefly went into coaching. He died aged 83 in 1958 and in 2004 his 98 year old daughter was present as he was inducted into the club's Hall of Fame.

1926
GOALS GALORE AND
RELEGATION

In 1925-26 Man City were one of the highest scoring sides in the First Division but ended up being relegated in addition to losing the FA Cup final.

In the league, City scored 89 goals, more than Arsenal who finished second. However their defence was poor and 100 were conceded.

Before Christmas they only won four games, scoring four in each of them, including an 8-3 win over Burnley. There were some heavy defeats as well, including an 8-3 loss at Sheffield United that saw manager David Ashworth resign soon afterwards. A team selection committee ran by the Board took over but City's inconsistency was highlighted on Christmas Day when they lost 6-5 at Bury.

The erratic form continued after Christmas and a 6-1 win over Manchester United at Old Trafford on 23rd January was followed by a 5-1 home defeat to Huddersfield in their next league game.

City did find their form in the FA Cup, reaching their first Wembley final and scoring 31 goals in just seven games on their way. In the third round they beat Corinthians 4-0 in a replay at Maine Road after a 3-3 draw, then overcame Huddersfield 4-0 in the fourth round. The fifth round saw a sensational 11-4 home win over Crystal Palace, then City beat Leyton Orient 6-1 away in the quarter final. City beat Manchester United in the semi-final 3-0 at Sheffield United's Brammall Lane, but they were beaten 1-0 by Bolton in the final.

They then had two league games left to avoid the drop and Peter Hodge was brought in as manager. He inspired them to a 2-1 win over Leeds at Maine Road but they lost their last game 3-2 at Newcastle, which combined with results elsewhere confirmed their relegation.

1927
DENIED PROMOTION IN LAST SECONDS OF SEASON

On the last day of the 1926-27 season Manchester City appeared to have done enough to win promotion only to be denied by a late goal over 200 miles away.

City had a good start to the season, losing only one of their first ten games and they led the table at the beginning of October. However an indifferent spell in November and December saw them fall to ninth by New Year. A three month, ten game unbeaten spell lifted City up to second by the end of March but they failed to build on this and drew five games in April.

It meant that on the last day of the season it was between City and Portsmouth for the right to join Middlesbrough in the First Division the next season. Both sides were level on points although Portsmouth had a marginally better goal average.

At Maine Road City thrashed Bradford 8-0 and looked to have done enough to go up, with Portsmouth winning 4-1 against Preston. However their game had kicked off fifteen minutes later and there was then heartbreak for City as Portsmouth got a fifth goal, meaning they now had a goal average of 1.776 compared to City's 1.770.

1928
BEST SUPPORTED TEAM
GETS PROMOTED

After the near miss of the season before, Manchester City made no mistake in 1927-28 when they confirmed their promotion with two games to spare and attracted more fans than anyone else in England.

City enjoyed a good start, winning seven of their first nine games to go top at the beginning of October. But a slight dip followed with just one win from five as they dropped to fourth. In December though, they really stepped into gear, winning six in succession which helped them to return to the top by the end of January.

On 24th March City won 1-0 at leaders Chelsea meaning it was very tight at the top, with just one point separating four teams. City were third on 46 points but had two games in hand on the other teams around them. City held their nerve and on 25th April went to Elland Road to face Leeds, who were already promoted and won 1-0 to secure their return to the top flight.

A key factor of their promotion was excellent home form, with eighteen out of 21 games being won. Due to their success, City attracted an average crowd of 37,468, which was higher than any other side in all four divisions of the Football League.

1928
ALL TIME LEADING
SCORER SIGNS

Eric Brook, the player who has scored more goals for Manchester City than any other, signed for the club in 1928.

Signed as an outside left (a modern day left winger), Brook joined City from Barnsley in March 1928 and scored twice in twelve games as City clinched promotion back to the First Division.

Despite playing on the wing Brook was a roaming player who could create plenty of opportunities for himself and others. In his first full season he scored a respectable fourteen goals while Tommy Johnson got 38.

After Johnson left for Everton in March 1930, City had their lowest goals tally since 1924 the following season, but Brook was the leading scorer with seventeen in all competitions. This was one of only two occasions in eleven full seasons with City that he was the leading scorer, the other being 1935-36.

As well as scoring plenty himself, Brook continued to create many opportunities for his teammates over the years, including setting up the winning goal in the 1934 FA Cup final. On the way to Wembley, he had scored a goal in the sixth round against Stoke described by many fans of the era as the greatest ever seen at Maine Road.

The Second World War ended Johnson's professional career, but his total of 178 goals in all competitions has not been surpassed.

1929
38 GOALS
IN 39 MATCHES

The club's record scorer in a single season is Tommy Johnson, who hit 38 goals in 39 league games in 1928-29.

An ex-shipyard apprentice, Johnson signed for City in 1919 and made his debut against Middlesbrough on 18th February 1920, scoring both goals in a 2-0 win. He didn't establish himself as a first team regular until 1922-23 and scored twenty goals three seasons running from 1925-26 to 1927-28.

In 1928-29 he opened his account with a goal in a 2-2 draw against Manchester United at Maine Road in the first home game of the season. Two weeks later he scored five as City won 6-2 against Everton at Goodison Park.

Johnson's only other hat-trick that season came on 29th March when he scored three in a 5-1 win against Bolton at Maine Road, taking his tally to 31 for the season. There were still seven games left of the season and Johnson struck seven goals in them as City remained unbeaten to climb to a final league position of eighth, after being fifteenth before the Bolton game.

Despite such a prolific season, within a year City's management had decided Johnson was past his best and he was sold to Everton for £6,000, playing for them against City in the 1933 FA Cup final. He also played for Liverpool and when his career ended he ran a pub in Gorton.

Johnson's record of 38 league goals has never been equalled by any City player and his overall league total of 158 is a record shared with Eric Brook, although Brook has scored more goals in all competitions.

1931
MANCHESTER CENTRAL DENIED FOOTBALL LEAGUE ENTRY

In 1931 their was the prospect of a third Football League club in Manchester but City and United joined forces to block the application of Manchester Central FC.

Central were formed by John Ayrton, a Director of City, in the days when there was no rules against having a stake in more than one club. He believed that there was a demand for league football in the east Manchester area that City had left behind after moving to Maine Road. They joined the Lancashire Combination and played at Belle Vue, one of the venues City had been considering when it was decided to leave Hyde Road.

A number of ex-City players were involved in the founding of the club, including former captain Charlie Pringle, while Billy Meredith was one of the coaches. The club got good crowds and finished seventh, second and seventh in their first three seasons, but applications to the Football League were unsuccessful.

In October 1931 Wigan Borough resigned from the Football League and Central, now in the Cheshire League, applied to take their place. Third Division North clubs were in favour of them joining. However City and United, who enjoyed reasonably good relations at the time, appealed to the league and received their backing. United were then in the Second Division and getting four figure crowds, so they were especially vulnerable to the development of a third league club in Manchester.

At the end of that season Manchester Central folded, their backers realising that the aim of bringing league football back to east Manchester wasn't going to happen.

1933
THE FIRST
NUMBERED SHIRTS

The first time Manchester City wore numbers on their shirts was in the 1933 FA Cup final against Everton.

City had a scare in the third round when they were held to a 1-1 draw at Third Division Gateshead, but they comfortably won the replay 9-0. They then beat Walsall 2-0 at home before wining 4-2 at Bolton in front of over 69,000 fans, with Eric Brook scoring a hat-trick. Second Division Burnley were beaten 1-0 away in the sixth round and in the semi-final City won 3-2 against Derby at Huddersfield.

Final opponents Everton had been Football League Champions a year earlier but were now tenth. City were sixteenth and no team were clear favourites, with the game being seen as a battle between Everton's flair and City's strength and determination.

Both teams wore their alternative strips to avoid a colour clash and for the first time, players wore shirt numbers to help with identification. Everton wore 1-11 with City wearing 12-22. City's numbers were in reverse order, with Brook wearing 12 and keeper Len Langford having number 22.

The game itself was a huge disappointment for City, who were outclassed by the Everton forwards and restricted to long shots by their defence. Jimmy Stein scored in the 41st minute to give Everton the lead and after Dixie Dean made it 2-0 seven minutes into the second half the outcome was inevitable. The final score was 3-0, James Dunn getting Everton's third ten minutes from time.

1934
ENGLAND'S RECORD CROWD
OUTSIDE OF LONDON

When 84,569 fans attended Manchester City's FA Cup sixth round tie with Stoke on 3 March 1934 it set a crowd record that has yet to be broken.

City were bidding to reach the semi-finals of the cup for the third successive season but needed a change in fortunes going into this tie, having lost their last three league games.

Such was in the interest in the game that the gates were locked before kick off with thousands still outside. Those lucky enough to make it in saw just one goal which came after fifteen minutes. It was a fortunate goal for Eric Brook, as Stoke's keeper thought his high shot was going over and left it, only to see it creep under the bar.

At the time, the crowd was the highest seen in England for a club game that wasn't a cup final. The staging of semi-finals and play off games nowadays at Wembley means that isn't the case any more, but it still remains the largest crowd at a match outside London.

KEEPER'S ERROR FORGOTTEN IN FIRST WEMBLEY WIN

FACT 32

In 1934 Manchester City overcame the disappointment of losing the FA Cup final a year earlier, coming from 1-0 down to win the cup for the second time.

City beat Blackburn, Hull, Sheffield Wednesday and Stoke to reach the semi-finals, where they beat Aston Villa 6-1 at Huddersfield. The final was against Portsmouth, who were eleventh in the league table, three points behind sixth placed City.

The game was played in wet conditions making the pitch very difficult and in the 28th minute Sep Rutherford's shot went under City keeper Frank Swift's body to give Portsmouth a half time lead. Swift, the youngest member of the team at just twenty years old blamed himself for the goal but was re-assured by Frank Tilson that they could still win the game and he would score two in the second half.

In the second half Swift made some good saves to keep Portsmouth at bay and in the 74th minute Tilson got the equalising goal from the corner of the six yard box.

With just two minutes remaining, Eric Brook crossed and Tilson converted to give City victory. His promise had been fulfilled and Swift's earlier error had been forgotten. Although it was City's second cup victory it was the first time they had won at Wembley.

1936
'FRUIT BOILER'
LEAVES CITY

In 1936 Matt Busby left Manchester City for Liverpool, having enjoyed eight years at the club after he decided against emigrating to America.

Busby came to Manchester from Scotland in February 1928 and signed a one year contract. At the end of 1928-29 he opted to stay with City rather than join his mother in America and made his debut as a forward on 2 November 1929 in a 3-1 home win against Middlesbrough.

By 1931-32 he was a regular in the side but had dropped back to midfield where he developed a reputation as a fine passer of the ball.

He appeared in the FA Cup final sides of 1933 and 1934 and also earned one Scottish cap, against Wales in 1933-34.

Busby's Scottish accent remained strong and when a census

compiler knocked on his door he was misunderstood and the official wrote 'fruit boiler' on the form instead of 'footballer'.

By March 1936 Jack Percival had taken Busby's place in the team but he still commanded a high fee of £8,000 when he was sold to Liverpool, where he became a key figure of their side.

After the Second World War Busby was offered a place on the Liverpool coaching staff but he declined this to return to Maine Road. Unfortunately for City it was with Manchester United, who were sharing the ground at the time and he went on to enjoy a hugely successful managerial career with them.

1937
FROM THE BOTTOM
HALF TO CHAMPIONS

When Manchester City first became League Champions in 1936-37 their success had looked improbable at Christmas when they were in the bottom half of the table.

Before the season started manager Wilf Wild sold Matt Busby and Sam Cowan, then spent £10,000 on forward Peter Doherty from Blackpool. City lost their opening game 2-0 at Middlesbrough but two wins meant they were top after three games. They then won just one from their next ten - a 4-2 home defeat against Sunderland left them languishing in sixteenth at the end of October.

They rallied briefly with four successive wins lifting them to eighth but a 5-3 defeat at Grimsby on Christmas Day left them twelfth after twenty games. However it would be their last defeat of the season. On 9th January City beat Manchester United 1-0 and spent the next two months gradually climbing up the table. On 13th February they drew 1-1 at leaders Charlton. It was their third successive away draw although they soon rectified this, winning 5-0 at both Derby and Liverpool, then 6-2 at Brentford.

With five games remaining City were in second place and on 10th April 74,918 saw them beat Arsenal 2-0 at Maine Road to leapfrog the Gunners and go top for the first time since September. Wins at Sunderland and Preston, meant a win over Sheffield Wednesday in the penultimate game would guarantee the title.

Against Wednesday Eric Brook scored twice as City made no mistake, winning 4-1 to leave them three points ahead of Arsenal. It completed a remarkable turnaround and Doherty's purchase was justified as he scored thirty league goals. There was an additional bonus for City's fans too as United were relegated.

1938
MOST GOALS BUT STILL RELEGATED

In 1937-38 Manchester City suffered a unique relegation when they became the first reigning Champions to go down, despite being the First Division's highest goalscorers.

There was no indication early in the season that City would struggle so much, as they were eighth after seven games. However a run of just three wins in fourteen games saw them fall to twentieth place on New Year's Day.

City's big problem that season was the defence. They scored eighty goals, more than any other side, but the 77 conceded was more than anyone else except for West Bromwich Albion, who were also relegated.

They also had a tendency to win by big scores then struggle for goals in other games. Derby were beaten 7-1 away on 29th January, but after that they won just one of their next ten games, managing two goals on just two occasions.

City sank into the relegation zone after a 2-0 defeat at Liverpool on 26th March but they climbed out of it by winning their next two games. It was extremely tight at the bottom and in their last home game of the season City beat Leeds 6-2 to keep their fate in their own hands.

Going into the last day of the season, just one point separated the bottom seven sides in the table, with City ahead of five other teams on goal average. City lost 1-0 at Huddersfield who guaranteed their own safety, but there was agony as four of the five teams below them won. This meant that City were relegated and to make matters worse Manchester United were promoted back in their place.

1938
TWO HAT-TRICKS
IN TWO DAYS

At Christmas 1938 Manchester City's Jack Milsom scored hat-tricks in successive days in games against Tranmere Rovers.

On Boxing Day City, who were eleventh in the table, travelled to Birkenhead to face bottom of the league Tranmere at Prenton Park. In front of 14,000 fans City recorded what remains their best ever away scoreline, as they won 9-3 with Milsom netting four. Ernie Toseland and Peter Doherty got two goals each and the other came from Alex Herd.

The following day the two sides met again at Maine Road, with the attendance of 43,994 being more than double the crowd for the previous home game. City again enjoyed a comfortable win, with Milsom hitting a hat-trick in a 5-2 victory, the other goals coming from Doherty and Jack Pritchard.

In total Milsom scored 22 goals in 35 appearances for City before his career was cut short by the outbreak of the Second World War in September 1939.

PROMOTED WITH RECORD
POINTS AFTER CHANGE AT TOP

FACT **37**

When the Football League returned following the Second World War Manchester City were promoted at the first attempt, as managerial changes saw improvement on the playing side.

City were unbeaten in their first seven games but three defeats from their next six left them sixth in the middle of November. At the time manager Wilf Wild also carried out administrative duties at the club, having responsibility for wages and ground safety in addition to team affairs. At his suggestion, he stepped down as manager and former captain Sam Cowan was brought in, but only for team affairs with Wild continuing a secretarial role.

The change had an immediate effect. Cowan's first game in charge was a 3-0 win at Newport, the first of ten wins in eleven games that took City top of the table, five points clear of third placed Birmingham. It was part of a 23 game unbeaten run that was finally ended on 3rd May when Newcastle won 2-0 at Maine Road.

The following week City got back to winning ways, beating Burnley 1-0 at home to confirm their return to the top flight with five games still to play. This was due to severe winter weather that had caused several postponements leading to the season being extended into June.

City's final game of the season came on 14th June when they beat Newport 5-1 at Maine Road to take their total points for the season to 62, their best ever haul under the two points for a win system.

Manchester City's return to the First Division meant they would be playing 22 league games a season at Maine Road due to the ground sharing arrangement that was in place with Manchester United.

United's Old Trafford ground suffered bomb damage during the Second World War leading to them sharing Maine Road while it was re-built, with City charging £5,000 per season plus a percentage of gate receipts.

When league football resumed the clubs were in separate divisions but City's promotion meant they would be facing each other in 1947-48. The first game on 20th September 1947 saw City as the home team and ended in a 0-0 draw, then for the return fixture on 7th April 1948, City were 'away' in their own ground. The game finished 1-1 with Billy Linacre scoring for City in front of 72,000 fans, 6,000 less than had seen the teams play when City were the home side.

The following season City were again home first on 11th September with United's 'home' game taking place on 22nd January. Both games were drawn 0-0, while this time the higher attendance occurred for the fixture where United were the home side – 66,485 compared to City's 64,502.

At the end of the season City chose not to renew the rental agreement and United returned to a part refurbished Old Trafford.

1949
FRANK SWIFT
RETIRES

In 1949 goalkeeper Frank Swift retired after seventeen years at the club.

Swift joined City in October 1932 from Blackpool and when regular keeper Len Langford got injured in December 1933 he came into the side after second choice keeper James Nicholls had a bad display in an 8-0 defeat at Wolves.

City lost 4-1 at Derby on Swift's debut on Christmas Day 1933, but the next day he kept a clean sheet when they beat the same opposition 2-0 at Maine Road. He kept his place in the side for the rest of the season as City won the FA Cup, having made just three reserve appearances prior to his first team debut.

Swift was a virtual ever present until the outbreak of the Second World War and he won the title with City in 1937. During this period he missed only one game, a 6-1 defeat to Millwall on 17 September 1938.

During the Second World War Swift guested for a number of clubs, including Liverpool and when league football resumed he was back at City as number one and also became England's keeper.

At the end of 1948-49 Swift announced his retirement, saying that he wanted to go out whilst playing at the top level. However when his replacement Alec Thurlow caught tuberculosis Swift agreed to help out and played four games the following season.

He entered a career in journalism and was regularly seen at Maine Road. He was killed in the Munich Air Disaster in 1958 when he had been one of the reporters accompanying Manchester United on their European Cup trip to Belgrade.

MAINE ROAD'S
FLOODLIGHT SWITCH ON

FACT
40

Manchester City's first floodlights were switched on for a friendly with Heart of Midlothian on 14 October 1953.

City were one of the first clubs in England to install lights, which at first could only be used for friendlies as their use still hadn't been approved by the Football Association or Football League.

The first match arranged took place on a Wednesday night against an emerging Hearts side who had finished fourth in the Scottish league the season before.

Hearts were no match for City, who won 6-3 with Bill Sowden, who hadn't featured for the side so far that season, hitting a hat-trick. The other goals came from Johnny Hart, who got two, and Ivor Broadis. There were two more floodlit friendlies that month, with Turkish side Fenerbahce being beaten 5-1 and then Celtic earning a 1-1 draw.

City were the first team in Manchester to install lights and when United entered the European Cup in 1956-57, they had to play their first game at Maine Road.

In 1964 the first floodlights were taken down and sold to non league club AP Leamington, with a new set of more powerful lights at the top of pylons installed.

1955
REVIE PLAN TAKES
CITY TO WEMBLEY

FACT
41

Manchester City reached the FA Cup final in 1954-55 after the adoption of the innovative 'Revie Plan.'

City manager Les McDowall was impressed at Hungary's tactics when they beat England 6-3 at Wembley in 1953 and his new system was based on their style. During 1953-54 City's reserves enjoyed a 26 game unbeaten run when they used a deep lying centre forward who dropped back to collect the ball, drawing the centre back out of position.

In 1954-55 McDowall used this system for the first team, with journalists christening it the 'Revie Plan' after City's centre forward Don Revie. The first game was lost 5-0 at Preston but McDowall stuck with it and City climbed the table, eventually finishing seventh.

In the FA Cup, City won 3-1 away against Derby in the third round, then beat Manchester United 2-0 at Maine Road in front of over 75,000 fans. Luton were beaten 2-0 away in the fifth round, before City won 1-0 at Birmingham in the quarter final. In the semi-final, played on a mudbath at Villa Park, City beat Sunderland 1-0.

Fans formed queues a mile long for tickets for the final against Newcastle who had already won the FA Cup twice that decade. It was not to be City's day as they lost 3-1 in a game that saw them reduced to ten men after 22 minutes when Jimmy Meadows had to go off injured.

Despite the cup final disappointment the 'Revie Plan' had on the whole been a success and Revie was named *Football Writers' Player of the Year.*

FACT 42
PLAYERS GET £5 AS CITY WIN CUP WITH INJURED KEEPER

A year after losing the FA Cup final Manchester City were back at Wembley where they beat Birmingham City 3-1, with the keeper playing on despite a serious neck injury and players getting £5 more.

City beat Blackpool 2-1 in the third round at Maine Road, before avoiding a giant killing act at Southend, winning 1-0 on a sand covered pitch. In the fifth round Second Division Liverpool forced a 0-0 draw at Maine Road, but in the replay at Anfield, City won 2-1, although had a stroke of luck when the referee blew the full time whistle just before a Billy Liddell shot went past Bert Trautmann into the net. Another Merseyside club, Everton were beaten 2-1 at home in the sixth round, then in the semi-final City overcame Tottenham 1-0 at Villa Park.

For the final, the Players' Union negotiated that each player should be paid £5 extra as the match was being televised live, a rarity at the time. City were still using the 'Revie Plan' and took the lead as early as the third minute, when Revie backheeled the ball to Joe Hayes who scored. Birmingham equalised in the fifteenth minute and then had two goals disallowed for offside before half time. After the break City took control of the game with two quick goals just past the hour mark from Jack Dyson and Bobby Johnstone, with Johnstone becoming the first player to score goals in successive FA Cup finals.

With seventeen minutes left Trautmann dived at the feet of Birmingham's Peter Murphy and was knocked unconscious. On being revived he insisted on playing on despite being unsteady on his feet and City's defenders kept the ball away as much as possible. As City collected the cup Prince Phillip commented that his neck looked crooked and subsequent examination revealed he had broken a bone in it.

FACT 43

1958
100 GOALS FOR
AND AGAINST

In 1957-58 Manchester City became the first team to both score and concede 100 goals in a season where they finished fifth in the league. Their 104 goals scored being more than anybody else, but the 100 conceded also making them have a worse defence than all other teams except Leicester, who let in 112.

An indication of how things would become occurred in the opening game, in which City came from 2-0 down to beat Chelsea 3-2 at Stamford Bridge. In their next game they lost 4-1 at Manchester United and towards the end of September a new tactic, the 'Marsden Plan' was adopted. This involved using Keith Marsden as an extra defender but after 6-1 and 9-2 defeats in successive weeks against Preston and West Bromwich Albion, the plan was dropped.

The re-adoption of the 'Revie Plan' saw City beat Tottenham 5-1 at Maine Road the following week, with home form remaining good as they lost just once in twelve home games before New Year. Away from home though they were inconsistent and lost four in succession in January and February, including an 8-4 defeat at Leicester.

City's lowest scoring game was on 29th March, when they beat Leeds 1-0 at home and the 100th goal came in a 5-2 win at Everton. In their last match Aston Villa won 2-1 at Maine Road, which took the goals against tally up to 100.

Over the course of the season City only failed to score in one game, a 4-0 defeat at Birmingham on 5th October, while in 24 successive games starting with a 4-3 win over Leicester on 12th October and ending with a 3-3 draw at Wolves on 22nd March, they both scored and conceded in every game.

1960
CITY END RECORD
WINNING RUN

The best winning start to a season in the top flight of English football was Tottenham Hotspur's eleven match sequence in 1960-61, a run that was ended by Manchester City on 10 October 1960.

Spurs scored 36 goals as they won their first eleven games, while City had a reasonable start and were eighth in the table before this game, having played only ten times.

The match was played on a Monday night at White Hart Lane and Bobby Smith headed Spurs into the lead in the 26th minute. However, five minutes into the second half Bobby Hayes set up Clive Colbridge for City's equaliser.

Spurs appeared nervous and didn't play as flowingly as they could, testing keeper Bert Trautmann only with long shots which he held easily. City then almost snatched a winner ten minutes from full time but Colin Barlow fired over the bar from close range.

Tottenham remained top of the league all season and also won the FA Cup, while City finished thirteenth.

In the game at Maine Road Spurs won 1-0.

1961
DENIS LAW'S SIX GOALS
STILL DON'T WIN TIE

In an FA Cup fourth round tie in 1960-61 Denis Law scored six goals against Luton only for the game to be abandoned and City lose the re-arranged game.

Law had been signed from Huddersfield Town the previous summer for a British record fee of £55,000 and soon started to repay that, scoring twelve times before New Year.

In the third round City drew twice with fellow First Division side Cardiff before beating them 2-0 in the second replay at Arsenal's old Highbury ground, with Law scoring one of the goals. In the fourth round, they were d r a w n against

Second Division Luton, with over 23,000 fans braving the weather at their Kenilworth Road ground.

On 28 January 1961 Law was in devastating form and scored all of City's goals as they raced into a 6-2 lead in the second half. However a downpour turned the pitch, which had been a mudbath at the start of the game, into a series of small lakes.

After 69 minutes the referee abandoned the game and it was re-arranged for the following Wednesday. Law, who was forced to pull out of the Scotland side who had a trial game on the same night, was again on target but that wasn't enough as Luton won 3-1 to dump City out of the cup.

Law never scored four goals again for the rest of his career, which the following summer took him to Torino in Italy and later to Manchester United and then back to Maine Road in the 1970s.

1962
CITY'S
YOUNGEST PLAYER

In 1961-62 Glyn Pardoe became the club's youngest player, making his debut before his sixteenth birthday.

Having grown up in Winsford, Pardoe joined as an amateur in 1961 and was selected as a centre forward against Birmingham at Maine Road on 11 April 1962, aged just fifteen years and 314 days. City lost 4-1, but he retained his place in the team for the next two games and was in the line up for the opening game of the next season against Wolves, which City lost 8-1.

Pardoe made only a handful more appearances in 1962-63 as City were relegated. He was in and out of the team in 1963-64, but played in the FA Youth Cup final against Manchester United, which City lost 8-4 on aggregate.

In 1965-66 Pardoe was back in the side as a regular, mainly playing in attack as City were promoted. The following season he was used as an emergency left back against Spurs in October due to injuries to Bobby Kennedy and David Connor. He performed well enough to establish himself in that role for the rest of the season and the majority of his City career.

Pardoe won the Football League Championship, FA Cup and European Cup Winners Cup with City, as well as the League Cup in which he scored the winning goal against West Bromwich Albion in the 1970 final.

In December 1970 he suffered a serious leg injury in the Manchester derby which kept him out of the side for nearly two years. When he returned to fitness Willie Donachie was the regular left back and he made only fleeting appearances, mainly at right back, before retiring in 1976 and joining the coaching staff. He now works in media.

1963
MANAGER RESIGNS
AFTER RELEGATION

City were relegated on the last day of the 1962-63 season, bringing to an end Les McDowall's thirteen year management spell at the club.

The season got off to the worse possible start as City were thrashed 8-1 at Wolves on the opening day, then after a 2-2 home draw with newly promoted Liverpool they lost their next three games.

City had started with Glyn Pardoe in attack but they then paid Scottish club Third Lanark £19,500 for Alex Harley, who scored both goals in the first win of the season - 2-1 against Ipswich at Maine Road on 5th September. Harley scored 23 league goals that season but it wasn't enough to help save City from the drop.

The week after the Ipswich game came a 6-1 defeat at home to West Ham - Keeper Bert Trautmann was sent off for kicking the ball at the referee. They sank to the bottom with a 1-0 home defeat to Blackburn on 29th September, but then went five games unbeaten and by Christmas had climbed to eighteenth.

Severe winter weather meant that City didn't play a single league game for two whole months. When they were back playing regularly again in March they struggled, losing six straight games to drop back into the relegation zone. They briefly rallied over Easter, winning two and drawing one but they then had five straight defeats.

In the last home game against Manchester United, who were also in trouble, City could only manage a 1-1 draw meaning their fate was out of their hands going into the last day of the season. City needed to better Birmingham's result to stay up, but lost 6-1 at West Ham to confirm their relegation. Just over a week later McDowall resigned and was replaced by his assistant George Poyser.

1964
BERT TRAUTMANN
RETIRES

In 1964 Trautmann retired after fifteen years and over 500 appearances at the club.

A prisoner of war who refused repatriation on release, Trautmann worked on a farm near Ashton-in-Makerfield and played part time for St Helens Town, before signing for City in October 1949. The signing of a German was not popular and led to a lot of protests, but he eventually won fans round with his performances. He was an excellent shot stopper who also saved more than half of the penalties he faced.

The 'Revie Plan' made use of Trautmann's throwing ability, as he started attacks by throwing the ball out to the wingers rather than kicking it as far up the field as possible.

Although city lost the 1955 FA Cup final he was a hero the following year when he played on despite breaking a bone in his neck.

Recovery from the injury led to Trautmann missing a large part of the following season and after his return he lacked confidence on occasions, a part factor in City conceding 100 goals in 1957-58. By the time he retired in 1964 he had played 508 league games although his decision to remain playing in England prevented West German selectors calling him up for internationals.

Trautmann's last game at Maine Road was his testimonial, in which a combined Manchester City and United XI took on an England side in front of 47,000 fans.

He later went into coaching, managing Stockport County, Burma and Tanzania before settling in Spain. He remained close to City, opening the new Kippax Stand in 1995, watching them on television and visiting a match as recently as 2010.

He died at his home in Spain on 19 July 2013 at the age of 89.

1965
CITY'S LOWEST
HOME ATTENDANCE

The club's lowest attendance for a league game at Maine Road was on 16 January 1965 when just 8,015 turned out to see a 2-1 defeat against Swindon Town.

City hadn't won at home for two months and were ninth in the table, well out of the promotion picture. Three days earlier they had been the victims of an FA Cup shock, losing a replay 3-1 at Third Division Shrewsbury.

The visit of Swindon, who were struggling near the bottom and brought no more than a handful of fans, hardly captured the imagination on a cold, damp and misty day on which some of the buses weren't running.

Future Maine Road legend Mike Summerbee was playing as centre forward for Swindon and he scored the second goal as they condemned City to a 2-1 defeat.

The following game saw a bigger gate as 11,931 turned out to see City beat Swansea 1-0. The dwindling crowds did make the Board sit up and take notice. At the end of the season Swindon were relegated and Summerbee signed by City for £31,000, which helped turn the tide and lead to a glorious period over the next five years.

1965
CITY'S FIRST SUBSTITUTE

The first time Manchester City used a substitute in a competitive game was on 30 August 1965 when Roy Cheetham replaced Mike Summerbee in a Second Division match at Wolves.

Substitutes had been allowed since the start of the season and for the first three games Glyn Pardoe, Bobby Kennedy and Cliff Sear sat on the bench without getting onto the pitch as the rules stated that they could only be made in the event of injury.

At Molineux, Summerbee was tackled near the touchline and went into the stand, suffering a cut to his face that required hospital treatment. Cheetham, a winger who had been at the club for nine years, came on in his place and City went on to win the game 4-2.

Cheetham also came on the next time City made use of the rule, in a 3-3 draw at Norwich on 15th September and in total six different players made substitute appearances that season.

Cheetham remained at City for two more years as a squad player, making three appearances in the title winning season of 1967-68 before moving to the North American Soccer League to play for Detroit Cougars. Since 2007 he has been treasurer of the Former Players Association.

1966
PROMOTION AGAINST
DOCTOR'S ORDERS

City returned to the First Division in 1965-66 after new manager Joe Mercer took the job against medical advice.

In April 1965 George Poyser was dismissed and was replaced by Mercer, who had won promotion and the League Cup as manager of Aston Villa earlier in the decade.

The previous year Mercer's contract had been terminated by Villa after he suffered a stroke and he took the City job against the advice of his doctor, who did concede that if he died then it would be doing the job he loves. Mercer appointed a young Malcolm Allison as his assistant. The Board backed them with money for new signings. Mike Summerbee arrived before the season started and George Heslop joining from Everton in September.

The exciting style of play, coupled with results soon brought the fans back and City lost only one of their first fifteen matches. On New Year's Day they beat leaders Huddersfield 2-0 at Maine Road in front of over 47,000 fans, leaving them third but just a point off the top with a game in hand. City then lost only one of their last twenty games and as they closed in on promotion midfielder Colin Bell was signed from Bury for £45,000.

City had the second meanest defence in the division, while in attack they were not over reliant on any one player, with leading scorer Neil Young only netting fourteen. There was also a good FA Cup run, as City knocked out First Division Leicester and Blackpool before eventually succumbing to Everton in a sixth round 2nd replay.

Promotion was secured when City won 1-0 at Rotherham in the fourth from last game and they remained unbeaten afterwards to go up as Champions.

1967
BALLET
ON ICE

One of Manchester City's best performances of the 1960s was when they beat Tottenham 4-1 on a pitch that resembled an ice sheet.

The match was played on 9 December 1967 and despite the wintry conditions a crowd of 35,792 turned out, higher than many others at Maine Road so far that season.

After the pitch inspection, City's players made adjustments to their studs so they had a better grip on the thin layer of frozen snow.

When the game began they had no trouble adjusting to the conditions with Alan Oakes forcing a good save from Pat Jennings early on. However after just six minutes Jimmy Greaves gave Spurs the lead after the ball bounced favourably off the wall into his path following a Terry Venables free kick.

City didn't let that setback get them down and they put Spurs under relentless pressure, deservedly equalising after eighteen minutes when Colin Bell fired in from the edge of the six yard box. Jennings then made a succession of saves and City were desperately unlucky not to be ahead at half time.

Four minutes into the second half Mike Summerbee headed City into the lead. They continued to dominate with Neil Young hitting the bar. In the 64th minute Francis Lee's shot hit the post but Tony Coleman had the simple task of tapping in the rebound. With fifteen minutes left Young made it 4-1 after only been able to block a Bell effort into his path.

No other team could have lived with City that day and they would have got double figures if it wasn't for Jennings. The performance, which was captured by BBC's *Match of the Day* cameras, has since become known as 'Ballet on Ice.'

1968
CITY WIN LEAGUE IN
DRAMATIC FINISH

When City won the Football League Championship in 1968 they did so after being off the top for most of the season.

After finishing fifteenth the previous season just one signing was made during the summer - winger Tony Coleman from Doncaster. After a 0-0 with Liverpool on the opening day City lost their next two matches but then won five in succession, and were third in the middle of September.

Three defeats followed, leading to the club breaking their transfer record and paying £60,000 for Bolton's Francis Lee, one of a number of strikers that they had been watching. Lee's arrival inspired an eleven game unbeaten run in which he scored eight goals, lifting City to second at Christmas, a point behind Manchester United.

Two defeats to West Bromwich Albion saw City fall to fourth but they then had a seven game unbeaten run, hitting the top for the first time of the season on 16th March when Fulham were beaten 5-1 at Maine Road. Just two points separated the top four sides and the next week City lost 2-0 at Leeds, who replaced them in first place.

City had a crucial 3-1 win over United at Old Trafford on 27th March, but didn't return to the top until a 2-0 win over Everton on 29th April. The following week City won 3-1 at both Spurs and Leeds. The latter had a game in hand, lost against Liverpool meaning the title was City's to lose on the last day.

On 11th May 20,000 City fans travelled to Newcastle knowing they had to match United's result against Sunderland to be confirmed as Champions. City won 4-3, with United surprisingly losing 2-1. They were popular Champions, the media acknowledging they had played the best football over the course of the season.

In 1968-69 City won the FA Cup and Joe Mercer became the first manager to win the Football League Championship and FA Cup as both a captain and manager.

Mercer had captained Arsenal to title success in 1948 and the FA Cup two years later. City's 1969 FA Cup run started with a home game against Luton, who were beaten 1-0 in the third round. They then beat Newcastle after a replay and in the fifth round had a 4-1 win at Blackburn. Spurs were beaten 1-0 at Maine Road in the sixth round and in the semi-final City beat Everton by the same score at Villa Park.

City were strong favourites to win the final, as their opponents Leicester were battling relegation but some newspapers predicted that the heavy pitch could be a great leveller. City coach Malcolm Allison was forced to watch the game from the stands as he was serving a touchline ban.

Leicester had been expected to play a defensive game but they were more open than anticipated, with Glyn Pardoe clearing a shot off the line and Harry Dowd saving a blistering drive from Allan Clarke. Tony Coleman missed a great chance for City, firing over from the edge of the six yard box but in the 24th minute Neil Young gave them the lead, converting a Mike Summerbee cross.

Early in the second half Andy Lochead had Leicester's best chance but he shot over the bar from close range. City then went on to dominate the second half but couldn't find a second goal, the game ending 1-0 as City added the FA Cup to the previous season's title success.

The following day the team undertook a thirteen mile open top bus tour from Wimslow to Albert Square.

1970
TRIPLE DOMESTIC
SUCCESS IN RECORD TIME

When City won the League Cup in 1970 they became the first club to win all three of English football's main trophies within a three year period.

The League Cup had only been in operation since 1960-61 but the competition only really began to capture the imagination of fans after 1967, when the first final was played at Wembley and the winners were allowed into European competition.

City avoided an upset in the second round, winning 3-0 at Southport. They then beat Liverpool 3-2 at Maine Road. Further home wins over Everton and QPR set up a two legged semi-final with Manchester United. Both legs were played in December, with City winning 2-1 at home then drawing 2-2 at Old Trafford to progress to the Wembley final against West Bromwich Albion, which was played three months later on 7th March 1970.

On a pitch that was more mud than grass Albion took an early lead in the fourth minute through Jeff Astle but despite dominating the rest of the first period City couldn't find an equaliser. In the second half Mike Doyle did manage to score and take the game into extra time.

Glyn Pardoe was City's extra time hero, scoring from close range after Colin Bell had flicked on a cross. City's victory completed the unique achievement of winning the League Championship, FA Cup and League Cup in successive seasons, a feat that has since been matched by Manchester United and Chelsea.

When City won the 1970 European Cup Winners Cup, fans unable to travel to Vienna had to make do with the radio.

This was only City's second entry into European competition. The previous season's European Cup campaign ended early with a first round exit to Fenerbahce, but this time they beat Athletic Bilbao at the first stage, winning 3-0 at Maine road after a 0-0 draw in Spain.

Belgians Lierse were beaten 8-0 on aggregate in the second round but the quarter final was a much tighter affair, drawing 0-0 away with Portuguese side Coimbra before winning 1-0 at home. In the semi-final City played the away leg first, again losing 1-0 in Germany to Schalke 04 before winning the return 5-1.

City's final opponents were Polish side Gornik Zabrze, who won their semi-final against Roma on the toss of a coin after three games failed to produce a winner. Due to travel restrictions imposed by the Polish authorities, no Gornik fans travelled to the game. As the stadium had no roof the walk-up gate was affected by torrential rain. As a result the crowd was just 7,968, made up mainly of City fans. Those at home had to make do with radio, as the FA Cup final was being replayed that night and television companies showed that instead.

City were without the injured Mike Summerbee but took the lead in the eleventh minute when Neil Young scored from the rebound after Francis Lee's shot was saved. Two minutes before half time they double their advantage when Young was brought down in the area and Lee converted the penalty. In the second half Gornik pulled one back in the 68th minute but City survived their onslaught to hold on for victory.

CITY AVOID FINE FOR
WEAKENED TEAM

In an end of season game with Liverpool on 26 April 1971 both teams fielded a number of reserve players but City avoided any disciplinary action.

It was City's third from last match in the league that season and was played on a Monday night. It came just two days before both sides were in European competition semi-final action – City against Chelsea in the Cup Winners Cup and Liverpool against Leeds in the Fairs Cup.

City's line-up contained nine players who didn't feature against Stoke two days earlier, while Liverpool made ten changes. In front of just 17,975 fans – Maine Road's lowest league crowd of the season – City came from behind to draw 2-2, the equaliser coming from an own goal when Ian Mellor's goalbound header was turned into his own net by Ian Ross.

For the European tie against Chelsea (which City lost 1-0 to go out 2-0 on aggregate) only four players who appeared against Liverpool featured, but key players such as Colin Bell, Tommy Booth and Joe Corrigan were still missing.

When the Football League investigated the team line-ups they accepted the medical evidence that City provided regarding the changes, but Liverpool were fined £7,500.

1971

58 BANNED FROM TEXACO CUP FOR FIELDING WEAKENED TEAM

Manchester City may have avoided punishment for fielding a weakened team in a Football League game but the following season they failed to get away with it when they did the same in the Texaco Cup.

The Texaco Cup was a short lived competition for English, Scottish and Irish sides who weren't involved in Europe and carried lucrative sponsorship bonuses, a rarity at the time.

City failed to qualify for Europe for the 1971-72 season and entered the Texaco Cup, where they were drawn against Airdrie in the first round. The tie didn't capture the fans' imagination, with just 15,033 turning out for a 2-2 first leg draw at Maine Road, less than half the crowd for the previous Saturday's league game against Newcastle.

Joe Mercer made four changes to City's team for the home leg, but for the return at Broomfield two weeks later nine players who hadn't been involved in the previous league game were included in the starting line-up. 18,000 fans had turned out hoping to see players such as Colin Bell and Francis Lee and the changes made them hostile to City's young team as they roared their side to a 2-0 victory.

Competition organisers subsequently refused to return City's £1,000 entry deposit and they were banned from competing for two years. City did take part again in 1974-75, by which time a group stage had been introduced. City were eliminated, finishing third in a group that also included Blackpool, Oldham and Sheffield United.

In 1971-72 Manchester City striker Francis Lee set a record for the most number of penalties scored in a season that still stands today.

Lee scored a total of 35 goals, with fifteen of them coming from the penalty spot. Thirteen of those were in the league, one in the FA Cup and one in the League Cup and he didn't miss any.

Along with Colin Bell and Mike Summerbee Lee was part of one of the best front lines in the league, with City frequently in the opposition box. Lee was brought down for many of the penalties himself although some journalists mockingly called him "Lee Won Pen", claiming he went down too easily and dived on occasions.

Lee's penalties meant he had enjoyed his most prolific goalscoring season and it was the first time he had hit more than twenty goals since playing for Bolton in the Second Division. He left City for Derby two years later but was back as Chairman from 1994 to 1998. His penalty record has yet to be broken.

TOP AT THE END OF SEASON BUT CAN'T WIN LEAGUE

FACT 60

There was disappointment at the end of the 1971-72 season as City went top of the table after winning their last game, but knew there was no way they could be Champions.

It was one of the most exciting title finishes ever, with just three points separating the top four teams when each had six games remaining.

The last regular Saturday of the season was on 22nd April, when City beat Derby 2-0 at Maine Road to go top having completed all of their fixtures. Agonisingly though, Derby and Liverpool, who were both a point behind with a better goal average, were playing each other two days later. This meant there was no way City could be Champions, unless that game was drawn and Liverpool lost their last game at Arsenal 8-0.

Derby beat Liverpool then Liverpool and Leeds failed to win their last games meaning that Brian Clough's side claimed their first title as City dropped to fourth.

The final position was a bitter disappointment for City as they had looked favourites to finish Champions in March, when four straight wins opened a five point advantage over Derby although they did have two games in hand. One factor in the slump was the signing of Rodney Marsh, a maverick player who disrupted the team's rhythm.

During the summer Joe Mercer left the club, his relationship with coach Malcolm Allison having worsened since they supported different factions during a boardroom battle a year earlier. Mercer took over at Coventry and Allison was promoted to the role of manager, but he resigned the following March as results were extremely disappointing.

1973
GENERATOR HIRED
FOR MATCH

When Manchester City faced York City in a League Cup tie on 5 December 1973 they hired a generator to make sure the game could be played of an evening.

An energy crisis at the time meant that to reduce electricity consumption midweek games could not be played under floodlights. As a consequence when City travelled to face York at Bootham Crescent on 21st November, the game was played in the afternoon but it didn't stop York's biggest crowd for many years turning out to see a 0-0 draw.

The replay was scheduled to kick off at 1pm but with a low crowd feared City hired a generator at the cost of £1,000. This allowed them to use the lights without having to tap into the National Grid electricity supply. 17,972 fans turned out to see them win 4-1, with Rodney Marsh hitting a hat-trick and Francis Lee scoring a penalty.

City went on to beat Coventry and Plymouth to reach the final but at Wembley they were beaten 2-1 by Wolves.

1974
UNITED RELEGATED
REGARDLESS OF CITY VICTORY

FACT 62

On the final day of 1973-74 City beat United 1-0 at Old Trafford, a result which is commonly believed to have relegated United. However they would have gone down anyway even if Denis Law hadn't scored his back-heeled goal.

City didn't have the best of seasons themselves, spending it all in mid table and eventually finishing thirteenth. They also had three managers, with Johnny Hart resigning in November and then Ron Saunders being sacked in April, leading to former captain and backroom staff member Tony Book being appointed.

The first derby in February brought no joy, ending in a 0-0 draw with the main talking point being when Mike Doyle and Lou Macari refused to leave the field after being sent off.

United had been in the bottom three since New Year's Day and by the time the two teams were due to meet at Old Trafford on 27th April they were in deep trouble, three points adrift of safety with just two games left. An added twist was that City's side now contained Denis Law, who was back at Maine Road after being given a free transfer by United in 1973 after eleven years at Old Trafford.

With nine minutes remaining, a backheel by Law fooled the United defence and bobbled into the net to put City 1-0 ahead. He was so stunned at what he had done that he walked off the pitch and was substituted. However, even if United had won the game, they would still have been relegated as Birmingham beat Norwich on the same day to confirm their own survival.

Law's goal turned out to be his last action in major competition, as he retired before the start of the next season although he did play two Texaco Cup games.

MIKE SUMMERBEE
LEAVES

FACT 63

One of Manchester City's most influential players left the club at the end of 1974-75 after ten years.

Mike Summerbee signed from Swindon in the summer of 1965, following their relegation to the Third Division. In his first season at City, he was the only player to start every game as they were promoted back to the First Division.

Playing as a right winger, Summerbee was more of a goal creator than scorer. He scored 66 from 449 appearances but set up countless more, including the only goal of the 1969 FA Cup final against Leicester. He was a battler on the pitch and known for a fiery temperament with Francis Lee joking that he would get his retaliation in first.

Unfortunately in 1969-70, injury forced him off the field in the first half of the League Cup final and he

also failed a fitness test before that season's European Cup Winners Cup final, but was an unused substitute.

Summerbee's City performances gained him international recognition and he was part of England's 1970 World Cup squad. Off the pitch, he also engaged in a number of business ventures including opening a menswear shop with Manchester United's George Best.

After losing his place to Asa Hartford towards the end of 1974-75, Summerbee joined newly promoted Burnley and later played for Blackpool and Stockport. His son Nicky also played for City and he is now a club ambassador.

1976
OVERHEAD KICK
WINS LEAGUE CUP

City's second League Cup success in 1975-76 was thanks to Dennis Tueart's overhead kick against Newcastle.

City began the road to Wembley with a second round tie against Norwich, drawing 1-1 away before the replay was drawn 2-2 at Maine Road. In the second replay at Chelsea's Stamford Bridge City made no mistake, hammering the Canaries 6-1. City then beat Nottingham Forest 4-1, and the fourth round draw set up a Maine Road derby with Manchester United. City romped to a 4-0 win, but this was marred by a cruciate ligament injury to Colin Bell, which kept him out of the team for two years.

Mansfield were beaten 4-2 at home in the quarter final, and in the semis City faced Middlesbrough. They lost 1-0 in the away leg at Ayresome Park and faced an uphill task in the return due to injuries. However despite fielding a relatively inexperienced team which included youngsters Peter Barnes, Kenny Clements, Ged Keegan and Paul Power, City won 4-0 to reach Wembley.

In the final against Newcastle, City took the lead after eleven minutes, Barnes scrambling the ball in from the edge of the six yard box. Newcastle equalised after 35 minutes but shortly after half time Tueart scored a stunning goal to restore City's lead. Willie Donnachie crossed from the left and Tommy Booth headed it towards Tueart who had his back to goal ten yards out. His overhead kick thundered in to the corner of the net, giving keeper Mike Mahoney no chance.

Tueart later said it was the best goal he had ever scored. Barnes was named *PFA Young Player of the Year*. However it was to be City's last major trophy for 35 years.

1976
RECORD APPEARANCE
HOLDER LEAVES

The player who has made more appearances for Manchester City than any other left the club in 1976 following seventeen years at Maine Road.

Midfielder Alan Oakes turned professional at the age of seventeen in 1959 and made his debut on 14th November that year in a 1-1 home draw with Chelsea. He went on to play eighteen games that season and also played more than half the games over the next three seasons.

After City were relegated in 1963 he became a virtual ever present in the side for the next seven seasons. He played in all but one of the league games in the title winning season of 1967-68 (only Tony Book appeared in all 42) and appeared in the FA Cup winning side of 1969. He also played in both finals as City triumphed in the League Cup and European Cup Winners Cup the following year.

With the exception of 1972-73, when he was restricted to fifteen appearances, he continued to be a regular until 1976, appearing in that year's League Cup final. Despite being one of City's key players for so many years, he was never given an international cap.

Oakes left at the end of 1975-76 having played a total of 678 games for the club, with a further four as substitute. But his career still wasn't over and he made over 200 appearances in the lower divisions with Chester where he was appointed player manager within a few months of initially joining as a player.

1977
KEEPER'S 22
CLEAN SHEETS

In 1976-77 keeper Joe Corrigan set a club record which still stands today, keeping clean sheets in 22 of the 42 league games he played.

Corrigan had been at City for ten years although he had only become a regular in 1969-70. At the end of the previous season his goalkeeping ability was recognised when he made his first England appearance in a friendly against Italy.

City started 1976-77 with a 2-2 draw at Leicester but Corrigan kept the opposition out for the next three games, two of which ended in 0-0 draws. His best sequence over the season was in November, when he kept four clean sheets in succession while the most number of goals he let in, in any one game, was on 30th April, when City lost 4-0 at Derby.

Corrigan's goalkeeping gave City one of the meanest defences in the league, with only Champions Liverpool conceding fewer goals (33 to City's 34). However in attack City were lacking and scored fewer goals than any of the other of the top nine sides.

City finished second that season, just a point behind Liverpool and the nearest they had come to winning the league until 2012. Corrigan also kept two clean sheets in cup competitions and although his overall total has since been broken by Nicky Weaver and Joe Hart, neither of those keepers has managed 22 in the league.

Corrigan remained at City until 1983, his 592 appearances being second only to Alan Oakes and he remained in the game, coaching at a number of other clubs until his retirement in 2009.

1978
PLAYER SIGNED FOR
MEDICAL EQUIPMENT

One of the first foreign players to arrive in England was Kazimierz Deyna who joined Manchester City in November 1978.

Deyna was 31 years old and had captained Poland in the World Cup in Argentina earlier that year, having also won an Olympic gold medal with his country in 1972.

As was often the case in Communist countries, the best players were called up by State sponsored teams and Deyna played for Legia Warsaw, the club of the Polish army. When they agreed to release him, the £100,000 transfer fee was paid by City in a combination of US dollars, medical supplies, photocopiers and other electrical goods which were in short supply there.

Deyna made a slow

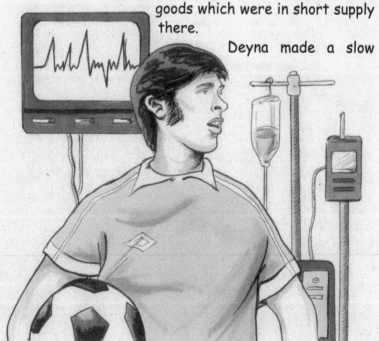

start to his City career but as the season went on he grew in confidence and scored six goals in seven games that helped City pull clear of the relegation zone. The next season, in which he suffered some injury problems he got six goals in 22 games showing some flashes of brilliance. On occasions though he couldn't keep with the pace of the English game and was playing passes that the forwards did not anticipate.

In 1980-81 he left to join San Diego Sockers in the North American Soccer League, remaining there for four years. He tragically died in 1989 in a car crash in California. His old Polish club Legia Warsaw have retired the number ten shirt in his honour and in June 2012 his ashes were returned to Warsaw for re-internment in a military cemetery.

1979
COLIN BELL
LEAVES

Colin Bell, regarded by many as Manchester City's best ever player, left the club in 1979 after failing to recover from a serious injury.

Originally from the North East, midfielder Bell scored 25 goals in 82 league games for Bury before joining City towards the end of 1965-66. He scored four goals in eleven games as they sealed promotion to the First Division, then in 1966-67 was an ever present as they consolidated their position in the top flight.

Bell combined speed with stamina, an unusual but effective combination. He was a member of the side who won four trophies between 1968 and 1970, earning a call up to the England squad for the World Cup in Mexico.

Bell continued to appear regularly until November 1975, when he damaged cruciate ligaments in a League Cup tie against Manchester United. This injury kept him on the sidelines for over two years and he eventually made his comeback as a substitute on Boxing Day 1977. His presence inspired the crowd and helped lift the team to a 4-0 win over Newcastle, the first of seven straight victories that saw City climb to second in the table.

Despite his comeback Bell was unable to rediscover his pre-injury form and just after the start of the 1979-80 season he announced his retirement from English football. He tried to continue playing for San Jose Earthquakes in the North American Soccer League, but made only five appearances for them.

Bell's total of 152 goals makes him City's third leading scorer of all time. The City of Manchester Stadium named one of the stands in his honour.

1979
BRITISH TRANSFER
RECORD BROKEN

In September 1979 Manchester City paid more money for a player that any British club had ever done when Steve Daley arrived at Maine Road from Wolves for a fee of £1.4 million.

The previous February Trevor Francis had become Britain's first £1 million player when he moved from Birmingham to Nottingham Forest, nearly doubling the previous record which had stood at £516,000.

Whereas Francis was an established England international, attacking midfielder Daley was still very much a player with potential, having only recently been awarded his first 'B' caps. With respect to the size of the fee City paid Malcolm Allison later claimed he only offered £400,000 and was surprised that Chairman Peter Swales needed to pay £1 million more, but Swales always denied this.

Daley never justified his fee, his ability to do so was not helped by the fact so many experienced players who he expected to be playing alongside had been sold to offset his huge price tag. The burden of being a British record signing was broken within weeks when Wolves signed Andy Gray from Aston Villa for £1.46 million, although he would remain City's record signing until Keith Curle arrived for £2.5 million in 1991.

After a return of just four goals in 47 games, less than half his goals per game ratio at Wolves, Daley was sold to Seattle Sounders for just £300,000 in 1981. He later returned to the lower divisions with Burnley and Walsall and now works on the public speaking circuit.

1980
ALLISON'S SECOND
SPELL IN CHARGE ENDS

In October 1980 Malcolm Allison left the club for the second time, having been in charge since January the previous year.

Since leaving City in 1972 Allison had taken Crystal Palace to the FA Cup semi-final and had a spell in Turkey managing Galatasaray. In January 1979, with City struggling in the league Chairman Peter Swales decided a change was needed and Allison was brought back as 'coaching overlord', with Tony Book's assistant Bill Taylor leaving the club.

City finished fifteenth in the league and suffered disappointment in the UEFA Cup, losing in the fourth round to Borussia Monchengladbach. During the summer Book was then moved into a general manager role and Allison promoted to team manager.

Allison set about moving on some of the more experienced players such as Mick Channon, Asa Hartford and Gary Owen, but big money was spent on young potential that didn't adequately replace them. Results were disappointing and City hovered near the relegation zone, then had a humiliating FA Cup third round exit at Halifax.

With four games to go City were nineteenth in the table, five points above the relegation zone. Three wins from their last four fixtures guaranteed survival, but Swales insisted that he would not allow such wholesale changes again.

Allison remained in position for the start of 1980-81 but after City failed to win any of their first nine games he left by mutual consent to be replaced by John Bond. Although Allison's two spells in total control of the team failed to work out as hoped, his time as Joe Mercer's coach, when he was very much the public face of the management team, means he remains fondly remembered by fans.

1981
THE FIRST WEMBLEY
FA CUP FINAL REPLAY

When City reached the 1980-81 FA Cup final they drew 1-1 with Tottenham Hotspur, leading to the first replay at Wembley.

John Bond took over a side that was second from bottom of the league. By January they had climbed to the top half of the table although they would eventually finish twelfth in addition to having the memorable cup run.

City beat Crystal Palace 4-0 at home in the third round, then hammered Bond's old club Norwich 6-0. An upset was avoided in the fifth round when they won 1-0 at Peterborough. In the quarter final Everton were beaten 3-1 in a replay at Maine Road after a 2-2 draw at Goodison Park.

City were handed a tough semi-final draw against Ipswich, who were second in the league at the time. However an extra time goal by Paul Power from 25 yards meant that City would be playing against Tottenham in the 100th FA Cup Final. After half an hour Tommy Hutchison, who had been Bond's first signing from Coventry the previous October, gave City the lead with a powerful header from ten yards. However with eleven minutes left he deflected a Glenn Hoddle free kick past Joe Corrigan and a replay was required.

The replay was the first for eleven years and the first time that one was held at Wembley. Ricky Villa gave Spurs the lead but City came back to lead 2-1 early in the second half. However with twenty minutes remaining Garth Crooks equalised and six minutes later Villa weaved his way through the City defence to score one of the greatest ever cup final goals. It would be thirty years before City appeared in another FA Cup Final.

1983
ENTERING DROP ZONE ON
FINAL DAY TO GO DOWN

FACT
72

After seventeen years in the First Division, Manchester City were relegated on the last day of the 1982-83 season, after they had been challenging for the title at one stage. City, like many other clubs, were in financial trouble at the start of the season. Trevor Francis was sold to Sampdoria for £900,000 after just one season at Maine Road and all the money from a new sponsorship deal with SAAB went straight to the bank.

Despite these problems there was no sign of any of the danger ahead as City won four of their first five matches and on 6th November - a 2-0 home win over Southampton left them second in the table, just two points behind leaders Liverpool. However they won only three out of the next thirteen, falling to mid table and after an FA Cup defeat to Brighton John Bond resigned.

Bond's assistant John Benson took over but he was unable to stop the slump, losing seven of his first eight games as City fell to within five points of the relegation places. By the time there were two games remaining, City had fallen into the bottom three for the first time but a 1-0 win at Brighton lifted them out of the drop zone and relegated the south coast club.

On the last day of the season, City were at home to Luton and needed a draw to stay up. However with just seven minutes remaining Raddy Antic scored for the visitors to ensure their own survival and condemn City to the Second Division.

CITY GET PORTSMOUTH
BACK 58 YEARS ON

FACT 73

City won promotion back to the First Division in 1984-85, claiming the final promotion spot on goal difference from Portsmouth, who had denied them in 1927.

Billy McNeil took over from John Benson after relegation but with little money available for new signings, City had to settle for fourth in 1983-84 in a strong Second Division that saw Chelsea, Sheffield Wednesday and Newcastle promoted. Prior to the start of 1984-85 Chairman Peter Swales stressed that City could not spend their way to promotion and the major summer signing was striker Tony Cunningham, who arrived from Sheffield Wednesday for £100,000.

City made a slow start, winning only one of their first five games but four successive wins took them up to sixth at the beginning of October. By Christmas City were handily placed, just a point behind third placed Portsmouth but they failed to take advantage, winning just one game from four over the period. City then went out of the FA Cup in the third round but this proved a blessing in disguise. With no distractions they won seven out of their next eight games, taking them top of the table, five points ahead of second placed Blackburn. However the pressure of being top seemed to get to the team and they fell to fifth after seven games without a win.

On 27th April City a crucial 2-1 win at fellow contenders Portsmouth, lifted them back into third place with three games remaining. A draw with Oldham and defeat at Notts County, meant that going into the last day of the season they were level on points with Portsmouth. However, with a better goal difference City made no mistake, winning 5-1 against Charlton to clinch promotion 58 years after they had been denied going up by Portsmouth on goal average.

1986
THE FULL MEMBERS
CUP FINAL

City's last cup final appearance at the old Wembley was in 1985-86 in the largely forgotten Full Members Cup.

The competition started that season, following the ban on English clubs in European tournaments and was only open to teams from the top two divisions. City were one of just five First Division teams to enter during the inaugural season, the format for which saw teams split into groups divided on a north and south basis.

The fans were hardly enticed by the competition and just 4,029 turned out at Maine Road to see them beat Leeds 6-1 in their opening game. They then beat Sheffield United 2-1 away to top the group and progress to the northern semi-final where they were drawn at home to Sunderland, winning on penalties after a 0-0 draw.

The northern final saw City take on Hull and after losing the first leg 2-1 they overturned the deficit with a 2-0 home win in the return in front of 10,180 fans, less than half the lowest league gate so far that season.

The final against Chelsea at Wembley was on Sunday 23 March 1986. It was deemed so unimportant by the football authorities that City had to play Manchester United at Old Trafford the previous day, a game that saw them come from two down to draw 2-2.

30,000 City fans then travelled to Wembley and Billy McNeil made just one change to the starting line-up, bringing in Mick McCarthy for Kenny Clements. Chelsea were fourth in the table and went 5-1 up thanks to a hat-trick from David Speedie. In the last five minutes Mark Lillis scored twice and had another shot deflected in off Doug Rougvie to give Chelsea an almighty scare, but a second comeback in two days was beyond them.

RELEGATED TWICE
IN A SEASON

FACT 75

In 1986-87 Manchester City were relegated in just their second season back in the top flight, with Billy McNeil taking both City and Aston Villa down.

Despite a promising opening that saw City beat Wimbledon at Maine Road on the opening day and then draw 0-0 at Champions Liverpool, they failed to win any of their next five games. Manager Billy McNeill then resigned, frustrated by the lack of money available to make new signings.

Assistant Jimmy Frizzell took over but couldn't stop the slide and at the end of October City were in the relegation zone, having gone twelve games without a win. They remained there until Boxing Day, when a 1-0 win over Sheffield Wednesday lifted them to eighteenth but two days later they lost 5-0 at fellow strugglers Charlton.

On 3rd January City beat Oxford 1-0 at Maine Road, which helped them up to sixteenth, but that was the last win in the league for over three months. They went fourteen games without a win, dropping to the bottom of the table. The arrival of striker Paul Stewart from Blackpool in March failed to turn the club's fortunes around. With four games to go City's position looked a lost cause as they were eight points from safety, but a 3-0 home win over Arsenal, 0-0 draw at title chasing Everton and 1-0 home win over Nottingham Forest gave them hope. On the last day they needed to win at West Ham and hope Charlton and Leicester lost, but a 2-0 defeat sealed their fate.

Also relegated were Aston Villa, who McNeill had taken over after leaving City. He was then sacked by Villa but went on to have success in Scotland when he returned to his old club Celtic.

1987
TRIPLE HAT-TRICK
AGAINST HUDDERSFIELD

On 7 November 1987 City had a remarkable 10-1 victory over Huddersfield Town, with three different players scoring hat-tricks.

City, now managed by Mel Machin, had only had an average start to the Second Division campaign and were tenth in the table, without a win in their last three home games. But Huddersfield were in an even worse position, bottom of the table without an away win.

Huddersfield were the better team in the early stages but after Neil McNab gave City a thirteenth minute lead there was only one team in it. The second goal came from Paul Stewart in the 29th minute and further strikes from Tony Adcock and David White gave City a 4-0 half time lead.

The start of the second half again saw Huddersfield begin well but Adcock got the fifth in the 53rd minute. Stewart made it 6-0 in the 67th minute and just a minute later Adcock, who hadn't scored for City prior to that day, completed his hat-trick for the seventh. In the 81st minute Stewart got his third and White made it 9-0 with five minutes to go.

Huddersfield had tried to continue playing a passing game rather than shut up shop and with a minute remaining got one back through a penalty from ex-City player Andy May after John Gidman had pushed David Cork in the box. City's fans continued to shout for a tenth goal and it came when White rounded the keeper to make it double figures.

Although this game will forever live on in the memory of those who were there, City were unable to win promotion that season, finishing a disappointing ninth.

1989
PROMOTION CLINCHED
WITH FOUR MINUTES TO GO

In 1988-89 City returned to the First Division although they made their fans sweat at the end of the season, before a late equaliser at Bradford confirmed their promotion.

During the summer Paul Stewart was sold to Tottenham for £1.7 million which funded the purchase of five new signings, including keeper Andy Dibble, defender Brian Gayle and striker Wayne Biggins.

City started badly, picking up just two points from the first four games but five wins out of six lifted them to fourth. They went top on 10th December with a 4-0 win over Bradford at Maine Road, but a disappointing Christmas period saw them drop down to fifth.

Mel Machin brought in Gary Megson from Sheffield Wednesday to strengthen the promotion push and he scored on his debut on 14th January when City beat Oldham 1-0 at Boundary Park. This was the first of five wins in succession that took them back to then top of the table at the end of February.

City remained in the top two and promotion seemed in the bag, but they wobbled at the end. In the last home game against Bournemouth they led 3-0 at half time, but ended up drawing 3-3, the equaliser coming in the last minute. This meant on the last day of the season City had to draw at Bradford to secure automatic promotion, otherwise they would face the lottery of the play offs.

At Valley Parade City fell behind to a Mark Ellis goal in the 24th minute and missed a host of chances in the second half. Crystal Palace were winning 4-1 at home to Birmingham, meaning one more goal for them would lift them above City into second place on goal difference. Eventually, with just four minutes remaining, Trevor Morley equalised to confirm City's return to the top flight.

1989
UNITED HIT
FOR FIVE

In the first derby after returning to the top flight, Manchester City hammered Manchester United 5-1, their biggest home win over their rivals.

City had won only one of their first six league games and a few days earlier suffered an embarrassing League cup defeat at Brentford, which didn't bode well as they sought a first win over United since 1981. They were also missing striker Clive Allen, a summer signing from Bordeaux.

During the summer United had broken the British transfer record to sign defender Gary Pallister for £2.3 million but in the eleventh minute he misjudged a cross and David Oldfield fired City into the lead. Soon afterwards Trevor Morley made it 2-0 and before half time Oldfield beat Pallister and crossed for Ian Bishop to head in the third goal.

Five minutes into the second half Mark Hughes gave United hope with a scissors kick goal, but Oldfield made it 4-1 just before the hour mark and four minutes later Andy Hinchcliffe's header put the game beyond doubt.

City's fans celebrated by chanting "Easy" and "Ferguson Out". The following week they beat Luton 3-1 but it wasn't to be the catalyst for a successful season. Mel Machin was sacked in November when City were nineteenth in the table. He was replaced by Howard Kendall and City eventually finished fourteenth, five points from safety.

The win was the first time City had scored five past United at home, having previously won 6-1 at Old Trafford in 1925-26 and 5-0 in 1954-55.

On 20 April 1991 City beat Derby 2-1 at Maine Road, a game that saw striker Niall Quinn score for City then save a penalty after he stood in as keeper.

Quinn had been signed from Arsenal in March 1990 and had scored some important goals that helped City pull clear of the relegation zone. In 1990-91 City were performing far better and although Howard Kendall stunned fans in December by leaving to take over at Everton for a second time, player-manager Peter Reid kept them in the top half of the table.

Against Derby Quinn gave City the lead with a left foot volley from the edge of the box, but later in the first half keeper Tony Coton was sent off after bringing down Dean Saunders in the area. With no substitute keepers then, Quinn volunteered to go in goal and dived to his left to turn Saunders' penalty around the post.

Despite being a player down City continued to dominate the game and David White increased the lead in the second half, although Mick Harford did pull one back for Derby and it finished 2-1. The win lifted City to fourth and they finished the season in fifth.

Quinn's feat has never been matched by any other player in England, although Paraguyan keeper Jose Luis Chilavert, who also took penalties and free kicks, managed it for Velez Sarsfield in 1999.

1991
ENGLAND'S MOST
EXPENSIVE DEFENDER

Prior to the start of the 1991-92 season Manchester City broke their own transfer record as Keith Curle became England's most expensive defender.

After the fifth place finish in 1990-91 the Board backed Peter Reid financially and the £2.5 million paid to Wimbledon for Curle was the highest that had been paid for an English defender by a British club.

Curle was immediately handed the captaincy and City began the season well with three straight wins. A bad September though saw them lose four out of six games. However they recovered from this, winning their next four games and they remained in the top six for the rest of the season.

Notable performances included a 4-0 win over eventual Champions Leeds, a 1-1 draw at Manchester United and 5-2 win at Oldham on the last day of the season.

City finished fifth for the second year running in what was the old First Division's last season before the creation of the Premiership. It may have been better had it not been for City's away form, as they went eleven games without a win on their travels at one point.

Curle's performances that season earned him a first England cap in April and he stayed at City until 1996 when he left for Wolverhampton Wanderers in a £650,000 deal.

1995
THE PREMIERSHIP'S
OLDEST PLAYER

At the end of 1994-95 Manchester City keeper John Burridge became the oldest player to appear in the Premiership, a record that has yet to be broken.

The much travelled Burridge had been signed as back-up to Tony Coton and Andy Dibble earlier in the season by Brian Horton, who replaced Peter Reid as manager in 1993.

On 29 April 1995 Burridge came on as a substitute for the injured Coton in a 0-0 draw with Newcastle at Maine Road. He then appeared in goal for the final three games of the season. The last of these was against Queens Park Rangers, who won 3-2 at Maine Road on 14th May.

The QPR game was Burridge's last for City and at 43 years, 162 days it made him the clubs oldest player since the Second World War and the oldest to appear in the Premiership.

The following season Burridge played what turned out to be his last games in English professional football for Darlington. He eventually retired in 1997, having been at 29 clubs in a thirty year career. After a spell coaching in Oman he now works as a television pundit in Dubai.

1995
ENGLAND'S
TALLEST STAND

In 1995 the new Kippax stand opened at Maine Road. At the time it was the tallest stand at an English ground.

To comply with the requirements of the Taylor Report, which called for all grounds in the top two divisions to become all seater, City started off by re-building the Platt Lane stand in 1992, part of a £40 million redevelopment plan that would lead to a capacity of 45,000.

The next part of the development was the Kippax terrace, which had been re-named from the Popular side in the 1950s when a roof was added. This was closed after the last home game of 1993-94 against Chelsea on 30th April, which ended in a 2-2 draw and temporary seating was in place during the construction of the new stand.

The new Kippax stand cost a massive £16 million to build, which was four times the club's annual turnover. It had three tiers and a capacity of 11,000, compared to the 18,300 that could stand on the terrace. It was the tallest stand in England at the time and the equivalent of a twelve storey building, with the third tier hanging from the roof.

It was officially opened by Bert Trautmann prior to the match with Aston Villa on 25th November, which City won 1-0.

The Kippax would be used for just eight years though, with the rest of the re-development being put on hold as City struggled on the pitch and they were then offered the chance of a move to a purpose built stadium.

1996
GEORGIAN PAIR FAIL TO SAVE CITY FROM THE DROP

City suffered relegation in 1995-96 after two Georgian signings were not enough to keep them in the top flight.

At the end of 1994-95 Brian Horton was sacked and fans hoped that Francis Lee, who had been Chairman since 1994, would be able to attract a big name manager to the club. However the appointment of Alan Ball, who had endured difficult spells earlier in the decade with Stoke and Blackpool, wasn't met with much approval by fans.

The big summer signing was Georgian Georgi Kinkladze, who arrived from Dinamo Tblisi for £2 million, although work permit issues meant he was unable to appear in any pre-season matches. City then had a terrible start, picking up two points in their first eleven games.

City turned the corner in November, winning four and drawing one from five games. Kinkladze's form was also improving after his mother moved to Manchester to help him overcome homesickness. His brilliant runs, ball control and finishing made him a favourite with the fans. His first goal for the club was in the 1-0 win over Aston Villa when the Kippax stand was opened on 25th November, a win that lifted City out of the bottom three for the first time.

On 16th March Kinkladze scored one of the best goals ever seen at Maine Road, beating five players then chipping the keeper in a 2-1 win over Southampton. Also that month his international teammate Mikhail Kavelashvili arrived from Spartak Vladikavkaz.

Kavelashvili scored on his debut against Manchester United, a game City lost 3-2 and it would be his only goal of the season. City went into the last day of the season knowing they had to better the results of Southampton and Coventry to survive, but a 2-2 draw with Liverpool condemned them to relegation.

1997
FIFTH MANAGER OF THE SEASON
GUIDES CITY TO SAFETY

In their first season back in the second tier since 1989, City failed to make a promotion challenge and relegation looked a real possibility as they got through five managers.

They were given a major boost before the season when Georgi Kinkladze remained at the club despite some lucrative offers from abroad. Alan Ball also remained as manager but although City won their first game 1-0 against Ipswich two defeats followed, leading to his resignation.

Ball was replaced on a caretaker basis by Asa Hartford, who won three and lost three games before reverting to a coaching role, as Steve Coppell took over in October. His appointment got a mixed reception as despite his managerial credentials he was an ex-Manchester United player. He remained in charge for just a over month, resigning on medical grounds on 8th November with City seventeenth in the table.

Coppell's assistant Phil Neal stepped in on a caretaker basis but won just two out of ten games as City sank to 21st place, just a point above the relegation zone. He was replaced on 30th December by former Nottingham Forest manager Frank Clark, who made some unpopular decisions including axing former captain Tony Book from the backroom staff. However, the team did improve under Clark and City were unbeaten in his first nine games in charge as they pulled away from the relegation zone, eventually finishing thirteenth.

Kinkladze was again named City's player of the year and was persuaded to stay at the club for another season, but his compatriot Mikhail Kavelashvili did not play enough games to get a renewed work permit and joined Grasshoppers Zurich on loan.

1998
RELEGATION DESPITE
TRANSFER RECORD

After having reasons to be optimistic at the start of the season City ended 1997-98 by being relegated to the third tier of English football for the first time in their history.

In addition to securing the services of Georgi Kinkladze City broke their transfer record, paying £3 million for Portsmouth striker Lee Bradbury.

Pre-season optimism was soon dashed as City failed to win any of their first four games and were 21st in the table at the end of October. Bradbury failed to live up to expectations and didn't score until his seventh game, managing just six goals in the league all season.

Frank Clark was sacked after a 1-0 defeat by Bury on 4th February and he was replaced by ex-City striker Joe Royle, who had enjoyed success as a manager with Oldham and Everton. Royle immediately changed City's style of play to a more defensive physical approach and saw Kinkladze as a luxury that couldn't be afforded in a relegation fight. The Georgian played only four more games all season, less than his compatriot defender Kakhaber Tskhadadze who joined from Alania Vladikavkaz. City won three of Royle's first five games in charge to move up to seventeenth, but a run of just one win in eight left them in the relegation zone with just two matches to play.

On 25th April Kinkladze was recalled to the side and scored in a 2-2 home draw with Queens Park Rangers, meaning City had to win their last game at Stoke and hope other results went their way. City won 5-2 but victories for Port Vale and Portsmouth meant they would be playing third tier football the following season.

1999
PLAY OFF VICTORY SNATCHED
FROM JAWS OF DEFEAT

City only spent one season in the third tier, securing promotion via the play offs in a dramatic finish at Wembley.

Despite all the suffering City's supporters had endured they stood by the club and the average attendance of 28,261 was the highest since 1981-82, even though they rarely looked like achieving automatic promotion.

Georgi Kinkladze was sold to Ajax and Bermudan striker Shaun Goater arrived from Bristol City. He finished the season as City's leading scorer, hitting twenty league goals but the main problem as a whole was too many draws. Sixteen games in all, more than all but two other teams in the division.

After laying twelfth in the table the week before Christmas, City went on a twelve game unbeaten run that lifted them into the play off positions. This included a 3-0 home win over runaway leaders Fulham and 6-0 hammering of Burnley at their Turf Moor ground.

But they had left themselves with too much to do. A 2-1 home defeat to Wycombe in the third from last game ended any lingering hopes of catching second placed Walsall.

In the play offs they beat Wigan over two legs to set up a final with Gillingham at Wembley. City seemed to have blown their chance of going up when they trailed 2-0 with just a minute to go. Kevin Horlock pulled one goal back then in the fourth minute of injury time Paul Dickov equalised to take the game to extra time. There was no further scoring and Nicky Weaver saved two penalties as City won the shoot out 3-1 to rescue themselves from possible long-term obscurity.

GOATER GETS
FREEDOM OF BERMUDA

City won back to back promotions to return to the Premiership in 1999-00, leading to Shaun Goater being awarded the Freedom of Bermuda.

Although Mark Kennedy arrived in a £1 million move from Wimbledon, Joe Royle largely stuck with the team that had won promotion, with nine of the eleven who started the first game against Wolves having featured against Gillingham in the play off final. City lost the opener 1-0, but a run of six straight wins took them top after eight games.

City lost their next two games, both away, at Ipswich and Norwich but they responded with six wins in seven and remained in the top two until the beginning of March. They wobbled briefly, falling to fourth after a 2-1 defeat at Barnsley on 11th March but this turned out to be the last of the season.

On 28th April there were celebrations at Maine Road as a 1-0 win over Birmingham meant promotion if they won their last game at Blackburn, although a draw would do providing Ipswich didn't win by nine goals.

City took 6,000 fans to Ewood Park although several thousand more managed to get into the home stands. In the first half Blackburn hit the woodwork on four occasions and took the lead three minutes before the interval. However Goater equalised on the hour and from then on there was little doubt about the outcome and they went on to win 4-1.

Goater finished with 23 league goals and he was awarded the Freedom of Bermuda that summer, with 21st June being declared 'Shaun Goater day' on the island.

2002
PROMOTION WITH A RECORD
POINTS AND GOALS TALLY

City's promotion of 1999-00 probably came too soon and they were relegated straight back to the First Division. However they bounced straight back again, breaking points and goalscoring records on their way to the Premiership.

Joe Royle was sacked after relegation and former Newcastle, Fulham and England manager Kevin Keegan appointed. City began the season in mixed fashion, winning six and losing four of the opening ten games. These included a 6-2 win at Sheffield Wednesday and 5-2 home win over Crewe, but also 4-0 defeats at West Bromwich Albion and home to Wimbledon.

In an attempt to find more consistency Keegan brought in Algerian international Ali Bernabia from Paris Saint Germain on a free transfer and he became a firm crowd favourite, being named player of the season. Christian Negouai also arrived and by November City had began to move up the table. A 1-0 win over Wolves on 11th December saw them leapfrog them into second and on New Year's Day they hit the top with a 3-1 win at Sheffield United.

Keegan's attacking principles meant the goals were going in and in the second half of the season they only failed to find the net twice in 23 games. After Christmas City were never out of the top two and won ten consecutive home games, scoring three or more goals in eight of these.

They clinched both promotion and the Championship with a 5-1 home win over Barnsley in their penultimate game. Their final points tally of 99 is a club record and the goals total of 108 matched that from 1926-27.

2002
LAST MAINE ROAD DERBY
RESULTS IN VICTORY

In the last derby at Maine Road, City beat United 3-1 to secure their first win over them since 1989.

2002-03 was City's last at Maine Road as they prepared to move to the City of Manchester Stadium, which was in the process of being converted to a football stadium after it had been the main venue for the 2002 Commonwealth Games. Since City had beaten United 5-1 in 1989-90 they had failed to win in seven attempts at Maine Road and were determined to put that record right in the last derby there.

In front of a fiercely passionate crowd City took the lead after just five minutes when Nicolas Anelka, a £13 million summer signing from Paris Saint Germain, scored from close range after Fabien Barthez had spilled Shaun Goater's shot. However within three minutes Ole Gunnar Solksjaer levelled for United after some hesitant defending.

In the 26th minute City were back in front after Gary Neville dallied near the touchline allowing Goater to dispossess him and score with a fine drive past Barthez.

Five minutes into the second half Eyal Berkovic played a glorious chipped pass to Goater who fired in his 100th City goal. Keeper Peter Schmeichel was in good form, denying his former teammates Solskjaer and Ryan Giggs as United tried to get back into the game. Gary Neville was jeered mercilessly by City fans until his torment ended as he was substituted after an hour, but his replacement John O'Shea was barracked when he spooned the ball high and wide in injury time.

The game was a memorable way for City fans to remember the last Maine Road derby as they achieved a first win over United in thirteen years.

FACT 90
TRAGEDY FOR CITY'S LAST MAINE ROAD SCORER

In 2003 City left Maine Road after eighty years to move to the City of Manchester Stadium. There was then tragedy in the summer when City's last scorer at the stadium, Marc Vivien Foe, collapsed and died during an international game.

City had a sound first season back in the Premiership, overcoming a poor run in September to eventually finish twelfth. They had an outside chance of European qualification at one point, although they did end up getting into the UEFA Cup through fair play.

The most memorable game at Maine Road was the 3-1 over Manchester United, whilst another great moment was Niclas Jensen's stunning volley in a 2-1 win over Leeds.

The last game at Maine Road was at home to Southampton on 11th May. It was preceded by several former players being introduced to the crowd. City were by far the better side but couldn't convert their chances and the Saints came away with a 1-0 victory.

City's last goalscorer at Maine Road had been Cameroon international Foe, who was on a season long loan from Lyon and scored the third goal in a 3-0 win over Sunderland on 21st April. On 26th June he was playing for Cameroon against Colombia in a Confederations Cup match when he collapsed suddenly on the pitch. Attempts to resuscitate him failed and he was found to have died from a previously unknown hereditary heart defect. Foe's number 23 shirt has since been retired by City in his memory and there is a small memorial to him at the City of Manchester Stadium.

The new 48,000 capacity stadium was opened on 10th August 2003 with a friendly against Barcelona. City won 2-1, with Nicolas Anelka scoring the first goal there.

2004
3 DOWN AT HALF-TIME
ENDS IN VICTORY

On 4 February 2004 Manchester City pulled off arguably the greatest ever FA Cup comeback when they won 4-3 at Tottenham after being 3-0 down at half time.

City were fifteenth in the Premiership when they travelled to North London for the fourth round tie, with Spurs two places above them. They fell a goal behind after just two minutes when Ledley King scored and in the nineteenth minute Robbie Keane made it 2-0. With two minutes of the first half remaining Christian Ziege appeared to put the game beyond doubt when he fired in a free kick.

City's cause wasn't helped when Joey Barton was sent off for dissent as the teams left the pitch at half time. Three minutes after the restart Sylvain Distin's header reduced the deficit. In the 69th minute Paul Bosvelt's shot made it 3-2 after it took a deflection off Anthony Gardner.

With ten minutes remaining Shaun Wright-Phillips equalised, latching on to a long ball but City were still not content to settle for a replay. In the final minute Jon Macken, who had come on as first half substitute for the injured Nicolas Anelka, got the winner with a looping header from Michael Tarnat's cross.

This was the first time a team had come from 3-0 down to win away from home in the FA Cup and had been made more remarkable given that City played with ten men for the whole of the time that they scored their four goals. The only other comeback from 3-0 down was in 2000-01 when Tranmere, who were the home side, came back to beat Southampton 4-3.

2005
RECORD OUTGOING
TRANSFER TWICE BROKEN

In 2005 City twice received their highest fee for a player as Nicolas Anelka and Shaun Wright-Phillips both left the club in big money deals.

Anelka was the first to leave in January, joining Turkish side Fenerbache for £7 million. The French striker had angered fans and manager Kevin Keegan by claiming in an interview that he wished to join a bigger club. In March Keegan left the club by mutual consent, having already announced his intention to retire anyway at the end of the season. He was replaced by assistant Stuart Pearce.

The £7 million for Anelka was the biggest transfer fee City had ever received, but in the summer Pearce then oversaw a transfer that brought in over three times that amount, when Shaun Wright Phillips moved to Chelsea for £21 million.

In both cases the money received didn't all get invested in the team but was instead used to reduce club debts. City still owed £5 million to Paris Saint Germain from the original purchase of Anelka in 2002 and he was replaced by Kiki Musampa, who arrived on loan from Atletico Madrid. Less than half of the money received for Wright-Phillips was put into team building, with Darius Vassell and Georgios Samaras arriving for a combined total of £8 million.

With the lack of significant team investment, the next two seasons on the pitch were disappointing as City finished fifteenth and fourteenth in the Premiership.

2006
PLAYER BOUGHT FROM CLUB
HE NEVER PLAYED FOR

In the summer of 2006 Manchester City signed Dietmar Hamman from Bolton, paying £400,000 for a player who had not even kicked a ball for them.

The former German international midfielder had been released by Liverpool after seven successful years there and signed a pre-contract with Bolton in June. However he then had a sudden change of heart and told their manager Sam Allardyce he didn't want to honour the deal.

Hamman agreed terms with City and Bolton, not wanting to force a player to stay with them against his wishes, agreed to the move but only if they received £400,000 compensation. Hamman signed for City on 12th July and although Allardyce was disappointed by his decision he admitted that it was the best bit of transfer business he had ever done.

Hamman stayed at City for three seasons, playing 71 games and scoring one goal, against Streymur in the UEFA Cup. After leaving he played for Milton Keynes Dons, had a brief spell as manager of Stockport County and now works in the media.

2007
THE FIRST
OVERSEAS MANAGER

In 2007 former England boss Sven Goran Eriksson became Manchester City's first manager from outside the British Isles.

City had a very poor season in 2006-07, only confirming their Premiership status with three games remaining and scoring just ten goals at home, an all time league record low.

Stuart Pearce was sacked and he was

replaced by Eriksson, who had been out of the game since resigning as England manager a year earlier. He had good club credentials, having won the Italian league with Lazio and the UEFA Cup with IFK Gothenburg.

Under Eriksson, City had a good start to the season and were third at the end of November. Although they did tail off to eventually end up in ninth, this was still within new Chairman Thaksin Shinawatra's target of a top ten finish for the season. However despite the support of fans, who wore Eriksson masks in the penultimate game of the season away at Liverpool, speculation grew concerning his future.

The uncertainty didn't help the players who were hammered 8-1 at Middlesbrough on the last day of the season. Eriksson remained in charge for a post-season tour of the Far East but after this he left by mutual consent, with Mark Hughes taking over as manager.

2008
FIRST DOUBLE OVER
UNITED SINCE 1970

In 2007-08 City fans finally beat United both home and away, completing the double over their rivals for the first time since 1969-70.

The first derby was early in the season at the City of Manchester Stadium and was the third game for both sides. United started the better and City keeper Kasper Schmeichel made two good saves from Nani but in the 31st minute Geovanni's shot deflected off Nemanja Vidic to put City 1-0 up.

City dominated the rest of the half but couldn't increase their lead. Micah Richards was a rock at the back as City held on for victory. The closest United came to an equaliser was a Vidic header that came back off the crossbar. It maintained City's 100% winning start whereas United had just two points from their opening three games.

City were seventh when the sides met again on 10th February, which was United's closest game to the fiftieth anniversary of the Munich Air Disaster. Both sides wore sponsorless 1950s style replica shirts and a minute's silence before the game was impeccably observed.

Darius Vassell opened the scoring after 25 minutes and then Benjani headed City's second just before half time. Dietmar Hamman almost made it 3-0 just after the break but his volley was well saved. City stifled United in the second half and they barely created a meaningful attack, Michael Carrick's consolation in the last minute being too late.

2-1 had been the same scoreline when City last completed a double at Old Trafford, the last time being on 28 March 1970 when Francis Lee and Mike Doyle were their scorers.

2008
HOME EUROPEAN
TIE AT BARNSLEY

In 2008-09 Manchester City began their European campaign with a home game played thirty miles away in Barnsley.

City had qualified for the UEFA Cup due to their fair play record, but with the first qualifying round being played in July the pitch at the City of Manchester Stadium was not in a playable condition due to a series of summer concerts there. City initially hoped to play at Preston but the police opposed it and Barnsley's 23,000 capacity Oakwell Stadium was chosen instead.

The two matches against Faroese side EB Streymur were new manager Mark Hughes's first competitive games in charge. City avoided an upset in the Faroe Islands, winning 2-0. In the second leg at Barnsley, City overcame a stubborn defence, with goals from Martin Petrov Darius Vassell giving them a 2-0 win in a game that was watched by a crowd of just 7,334.

For the next round against Midtjylland of Denmark City could use their own stadium again and after a shock 1-0 defeat at home, went through after a penalty shoot out in Denmark following a 1-0 win there.

City made it to the group stages with a win over Cypriot side AC Omonia in the final qualifying round and were eventually eliminated in the quarter finals by Hamburg.

2008
THAKSIN SHINAWATRA
SELLS UP

Early in 2008-09 the football world was rocked when Manchester City were sold to the *Abu Dhabi Investment Company.*

That year City's owner Thaksin Shinawatra was facing gaol in his native Thailand, where he faced charges of corruption, causing massive uncertainty around the club.

However behind the scenes negotiations were ongoing and on 1st September, transfer deadline day, it was announced that City were being sold for around £200 million to the *Abu Dhabi United Group for Development and Investment.*

City's new owners were reputed to be worth over £800 billion and made it clear they wanted to become the biggest club in England. As a statement of intent, on the same day City paid £32.5 million to Real Madrid for Brazilian striker Robinho. Although he scored on his debut against Chelsea, City lost 3-1 but the following week he helped the side to a 6-0 win against Portsmouth.

In the January transfer window City were linked to a £100 million move for another Brazilian, Kaka, but in the end their spending was much more modest, with striker Craig Bellamy arriving from West Ham for £14 million and keeper Shay Given joining from Newcastle for £8 million.

City finished in tenth that season, having been near the relegation zone in December, but there was the promise of more big name arrivals to come.

2009
TEVEZ WELCOMES
PEOPLE TO MANCHESTER

In the summer of 2009 Manchester City set about putting together a side that was capable of challenging for honours, with the arrival of Carlos Tevez being the signing that caused the biggest sensation.

City spent £100 million on players in total, with strikers Emmanuel Adebayor and Roque Santa Cruz arriving from Arsenal and Blackburn for £25 and £17 million, midfielder Gareth Barry from Aston Villa for £12 million and defender Joleon Lescott from Everton for £24 million. By far the biggest sensation though was the £26 million capture of former Manchester United striker Carlos Tevez.

Argentine Tevez had been loaned to United in 2007 by *Media Sports Investments*, who owned his rights. In 2009 however United attempted to make the deal permanent, but Tevez indicated he did not wish to remain with them. After turning down an approach from Liverpool, Tevez signed for City on 14th June, becoming the first player to move from United to City since Terry Cooke in 1999.

Tevez was given the same number 32 shirt he had earlier worn at United and previous club West Ham. City then took out a billboard in Deansgate, near the boundary with Trafford where United's stadium is situated, with a picture of Tevez and the slogan 'Welcome to Manchester'. Tevez scored 23 goals in 35 Premiership appearances in 2009-10 although City missed out on Champions League qualification.

In December with City sixth in the table Mark Hughes was sacked and replaced by former Inter Milan boss Roberto Mancini, but he could only guide them to a fifth place finish.

In 2011 Manchester City ended their 35 year trophy drought when they triumphed in the FA Cup, again winning the final on a day that league fixtures were also played.

City's run to Wembley had an unconvincing start, as they needed replays to beat lower league Leicester and Notts County in the third and fourth rounds. They then beat Premiership side Aston Villa 3-0 before winning 1-0 against Championship side Reading in the sixth round.

In the semi-final City played Treble chasing Manchester United at Wembley, where a goal from Yaya Toure was enough to win the game. It kept up City's remarkably good record in FA Cup semi-finals, as it was their ninth win out of eleven, but their first since 1981 and first time they had been involved in a semi-final at Wembley.

The final was on 14th May and for the first time since 1934, when City also won the cup, it was played on a day that league matches also took place. City's opponents in the final were Stoke, who ironically they were scheduled to meet in the Premiership on the same day.

City had the better of the game but the winner didn't come until the 74th minute, when Yaya Toure hit an unstoppable shot from ten yards after pouncing on a loose ball in the area.

Stoke resorted to long balls to try and get back into the game but City comfortably held on for victory and end their 35 year wait for a trophy.

The FA Cup win completed a memorable week for City as four days earlier they had beaten Tottenham to secure Champions League qualification for the first time.

After winning the cup, they won their last two league games to finish third in the table.

After a 42 year wait Manchester City were crowned Premiership Champions in 2012, the title clinching goal coming in injury time on the last day of the season.

City further strengthened their squad in preparation for a title assault with Gael Clichy and Samir Nasri arriving from Arsenal, but the highest profile signing was Argentine striker Sergio Aguero, who joined for a club record £38 million. City won eleven of their opening twelve games, including a stunning 6-1 win against Manchester United at Old Trafford. But that was United's only defeat before Christmas and despite a perfect home record at the halfway stage City only led the table on goal difference.

By the end of February City led by five points but a 1-0 defeat at Swansea, then a run of three games without a win left them trailing United by eight points with just six games remaining. United then wobbled and on 30th April City beat them 1-0 at the City of Manchester Stadium to go top on goal difference with two games left.

Going into the final day of the season, City knew a win at home against Queens Park Rangers would guarantee the title, providing United didn't win by a freak scoreline at Sunderland.

At half time things were going to plan with City leading 1-0, as were United. Then in the second half QPR, who needed a point to avoid relegation, struck twice and clung on even though they were reduced to ten men when ex-City player Joey Barton was sent off.

In the first minute of injury time Edin Dzeko equalised but the final whistle at Sunderland signalled

United were about to win a twentieth title. However less than a minute after United's game finished, Aguero struck in the fourth added minute to confirm City as Champions in the latest ever finish to a title race.

Sources

www.citytilidie.com
www.bluemoon-mcfc.co.uk
www.mcivta.com
www.mcfcstats.com
www.statto.com

The 100 Facts Series